Year-Round
Catechumenate

Font and Table Series

The Font and Table Series offers pastoral perspectives on Christian baptism, confirmation and eucharist.

OTHER TITLES IN THE SERIES:

Baptism Is a Beginning

The Catechumenate and the Law

Celebrating the Rites of Adult Initiation: Pastoral Reflections

The Church Speaks about Sacraments with Children: Baptism, Confirmation, Eucharist, Penance

Confirmation: A Parish Celebration

Confirmed as Children, Affirmed as Teens

Finding and Forming Sponsors and Godparents

Guide for Sponsors

How Does a Person Become a Catholic?

How to Form a Catechumenate Team

Infant Baptism: A Parish Celebration

One at the Table: The Reception of Baptized Christians

Readings in the Christian Initiation of Children

Welcoming the New Catholic

When Should We Confirm? The Order of Initiation

RELATED MATERIAL AVAILABLE THROUGH LITURGY TRAINING PUBLICATIONS:

The Rite of Christian Initiation of Adults (ritual and study editions)

Rito de la Iniciación Cristiana de Adultos (ritual and study editions)

Catechumenate: A Journal of Christian Initiation

Baptism Sourcebook

Access to the Sacraments of Initiation and Reconciliation for Developmentally Disabled Persons

Echoing God's Word: Formation for Catechists and Homilists in a Catechumenal Church

The Godparent Book

The Hallelujah Highway: A History of the Catechumenate

Liturgies of the Triduum (3-volume video series)

New Life: A Parish Celebrates Infant Baptism (video)

This Is the Night: A Parish Welcomes New Members (video)

La Iniciacíon Cristiana: Un Recurso Básico

Forum Essays Series:

    The Role of the Assembly in Christian Initiation

    Eucharist as Sacrament of Initiation

    On the Rite of Election

    Preaching the Rites of Christian Initiation

    Liturgical Spirituality and the Rite of Christian Initiation of Adults

    Images of Baptism

    The Reception of Baptized Christians: A History and Evaluation

Year-Round Catechumenate

Mary Birmingham

LTP

LITURGY
TRAINING
PUBLICATIONS

ACKNOWLEDGMENTS

YEAR-ROUND CATECHUMENATE © 2002 Archdiocese of Chicago: Liturgy Training Publications, 1800 North Hermitage Avenue, Chicago IL 60622-1101; 1-800-933-1800, fax 1-800-933-7094, e-mail orders@ltp.org. All rights reserved. See our website at www.ltp.org.

This book was edited by Victoria M. Tufano. Carol Mycio was the production editor. The design is by Lucy Smith, and the typesetting was done by Anne Fritzinger in Centaur. Printed by Sentinel Printing Company, Inc., in St. Cloud, Minnesota. The cover image is by Don Bishop © 1997 Artville, LLC.

Library of Congress Control Number: 2002141201

1-56854-412-X
YRCAT

CONTENTS

CHAPTER 1

Why a Year-Round Catechumenate?

Many people have been captivated by the vision of the year-round catechumenate as set forth in the *Rite of Christian Initiation of Adults* (RCIA) but are prevented from proceeding by the seemingly overwhelming and unimaginable challenges of implementing this vision. But appearances can be deceiving. Far from being overwhelming and unimaginable, implementing a year-round catechumenate is not only possible, but is also the best stewardship of the gifts and talents of potential initiation ministers. The purpose of this book is to tweak the imagination, suggest possibilities and reinforce a solid practice of initiation ministry.

To answer the question, Why do we need a year-round catechumenate? we must first make the case that one is needed—demanded, in fact—by the rite itself. As the church continues to grow in its understanding of the *Rite of Christian Initiation of Adults,* it has become obvious that the common practice of initiation in most parishes falls short of the vision set forth in the rite. We have come a long way, but the race has only just begun.

SUITING THE JOURNEY TO GOD'S GRACE

One way to answer the question, Why do we need a year-round catechumenate? is to pose another: Is your parish's process of initiation "one-size-fits-all," or is it tailor-made for those hungry seekers who come knocking at your door? The way in which this question is answered is the axis upon which the catechumenal process spins. In a one-size-fits-all model, very little attention is given to the baptismal status or the spiritual history of the seeker. The baptized, fully committed Christian who wishes to come into the full communion of the Catholic Church is treated the same as the person who comes to us as a blank slate as far as Christian faith is concerned. Is there something wrong with this picture? Certainly, yet this is the way things are in many parishes: John, the unbaptized, uncatechized inquirer, and Sally, the fully catechized, baptized, active Lutheran begin a nine-month program in September and embark on virtually the same journey culminating at the table at the Easter Vigil in the spring.

While this may be the way things are normally done in many parishes, the RCIA envisions something altogether different. The Christian initiation of adults (which includes children of catechetical age) is a "gradual process that takes place within the community of the faithful" (RCIA, 36) but respects the needs of each individual within that initiating community. It is "suited to the spiritual journey of adults that varies according to the many forms of God's grace, the free cooperation of the individuals, the action of the Church and the circumstances of time and place" (RCIA, 36.5). The journey must be tailored to respect the needs of each person who comes to us with his or her own history of God's grace in his or her lives. People come to us with different histories, and those histories are to be respected. Unbaptized, uncatechized persons and those who were baptized as infants but never again had further contact with a church community will need far different formation from those who were baptized and have lived a committed Christian life in another ecclesial tradition.

The RCIA addresses those needs specifically when it insists that, while those who are baptized but previously uncatechized may not have heard the message of Christ, their baptism affords them a different status: "Their status differs from that of catechumens, since by baptism they have already become members of the Church and children of God" (RCIA, 400). Their conversion is centered in the baptism they already received, "the effects of which they must develop" (400).

While respecting the status of such people, the rite insists that their journey parallels that of catechumens (unbaptized, uncatechized candidates for initiation) and that their process should mirror the catechumenate. They may benefit from the liturgical rites intended for catechumens and may need a journey of duration similar to the catechumenate. Catechumenal ministers must be mindful that such persons are already sacramentally one with us by virtue of their baptism, thus avoiding language and ritual practice that suggest that they are unbaptized.

The journey of unbaptized, uncatechized persons (catechumens) is to be long enough to allow the seeds of conversion to take deep root in the person. The bishops of the United States wisely suggested that the catechumenate proper is to last for a minimum of one complete year from the time the catechumen celebrates the rite of acceptance until their initiation at the Easter Vigil (National Statues for the Catechumenate [NS], 6) The formation of such candidates is based on the life and mission of Christ as it is celebrated in the liturgies and scriptures in one complete liturgical cycle. The baptized, uncatechized person may need a journey of similar duration.

The same is not true, however, when it comes to catechized, baptized persons from other ecclesial traditions. Such persons do need a process of formation, but the duration depends on the extent to which those persons have lived the Christian life. "Those baptized persons who have lived as Christians and need only instruction in the Catholic tradition and a degree of probation within the Catholic community should not be asked to undergo a full program parallel to the catechumenate" (NS, 31).

It is no accident that the RCIA does not specifically provide formation direction for baptized, catechized persons. The bias of the rite is that baptized, catechized persons need a different type of formation altogether. The National Statutes address this issue when they insist that those baptized in another ecclesial tradition should not be treated as catechumens: "Their doctrinal and spiritual preparation for reception into full Catholic communion should be determined according to the individual case, that is, it should depend on the extent to which the baptized person has led a Christian life within a community of faith and has been appropriately catechized to deepen his or her inner adherence to the Church" (NS, 30).

Besides uncatechized persons (both baptized and unbaptized) and baptized, faithful Christians from other ecclesial traditions, there is another category of persons who come to us: those who are unbaptized but fully catechized. They have lived a great part of their lives within the context of the Christian, and perhaps Catholic, community, but they were never baptized. Such people do not fit in the categories already discussed. Their formation, like that of the catechized, baptized person, is brief in duration and falls under the category found in RCIA, part 2, chapter 2: "Christian Initiation of Adults in Exceptional Circumstances." Their catechumenal process is abbreviated and parallels the sacramental preparation provided for baptized, catechized persons.

MAKING THE VISION PRACTICAL

What are the practical implications of all this for our parish catechumenate processes? This question, like the question at the beginning of this chapter, seems to be answered best by a series of other questions:

> — When folks come knocking at our doors, are we ready to invite them into our processes right then and there? We must take a serious look at programs that begin in September and culminate at the Easter Vigil nine months later. Such processes simply do not fit the vision that is set forth in the RCIA.

> — Do we provide a process in which the precatechumenate, the catechumenate and the period of

mystagogia are flexible, allowing people to move through the various stages as needed?

—Are our parishes prepared to celebrate the rites of initiation as they are needed? If we minister to people as the RCIA suggests, there will be more than one celebration of the Rite of Acceptance into the Order of Catechumens and the Rite of Welcoming the Candidates in a year, and there will be frequent celebrations of the Rite of Reception into the Full Communion of the Catholic Church.

—Are we prepared to minister to baptized persons according to their needs and not according to our own prepackaged programs? Some baptized people need only a few months of formation, while others need the longer period of probation suggested in the RCIA. As already mentioned, people who are somewhat catechized may be adequately ministered to in the regular parish catechumenal process.

—Are we open to providing a separate formation process for fully catechized people seeking full communion? Such persons may need only a brief preparation for celebration of the sacraments.

—Are we willing to develop the art of prayerful discernment in order to minister to each person who knocks on our doors seeking entrance into the Catholic communion?

—Are we willing to adapt our ministry to the needs of the diverse people with whom we minister? Is our catechumenal process culturally sensitive? Is our ministerial lens primarily white, middle-class and suburban when our ministerial reality is rural, Hispanic, campus-centered or another culture?

These questions require serious reflection. Is your parish ready for the challenges that the answers to these questions may demand? Perhaps yes. Perhaps not yet. But one thing is certain: God's Spirit always leads willing and open hearts. Perhaps now is the time to ask the difficult questions; if so, the time to make the decisions that the answers will demand will become clearer.

USING THIS BOOK

This resource aims to assist parish leaders making those decisions. The starting point for this examination of the year-round catechumenate is the theology that undergirds the initiation process. The principles discussed in this chapter will be explored in greater detail, along with the principles of liturgical catechesis, the practical aspects of the process such as ministry formation, administration of the rite, discernment issues, content of the various periods, and a review of the rites of the catechumenate celebrated in a year-round model of catechesis.

Practical hints will also be suggested to assist in implementation. There is, however, a hazard in providing such suggestions. People interested in moving to a year-round process often will say, "Just tell us how to do it." While that request is understandable, one person's recipe may or may not work in every pastoral situation. What works in a large, urban setting may or may not be appropriate in a smaller, rural setting. When parishes are immersed in the theology of the rite, however, the principles become the driving force behind implementation. Every pastoral practice must be judged in light of how it supports (or does not support) the vision of the rite. Thus, the suggestions found in this book are merely that— suggestions. If they are helpful, use them; if not, discard them and use something that will work for you. They are simply presented as a means of expanding the imagination.

This book assumes that the readers fall into one of the following categories:

> 1) A new vision of initiation has been suggested to the reader, and he or she is interested in learning more about it.
>
> 2) The reader is presently operating out of a nine-month, school calendar, religious education model of initiation and wants to know why he or she should consider changing.
>
> 3) The reader is convinced that the year-round model of initiation needs to be implemented in his or her parish and is looking for a resource to assist in that implementation.
>
> 4) The reader hopes to fine-tune the year-round model already in operation.

Regardless of how you fit within these assumptions, it is my sincere wish that this book would help every reader more fully appreciate the great treasure that has been given to us in the *Rite of Christian Initiation of Adults.* It is a masterpiece of grand proportions, one that has the potential to turn lives upside down, inside out and in the process make lifetime disciples.

CHAPTER 2

Sacramental Catechesis

S acramental catechesis is necessary to lead people to encounter and celebrate fully the sacramental mysteries they are preparing to celebrate. Two of the church's catechetical documents, *General Catechetical Directory* (GCD) and *Sharing the Light of Faith: National Catechetical Directory for Catholics of the United States* (NCD), point the way for this sacramental catechesis:

> Catechesis must promote an active, conscious, genuine participation in the liturgy of the Church, not merely by explaining the meaning of the ceremonies, but also by forming the minds of the faithful for prayer, for thanksgiving, for repentance, for praying with confidence, for a community spirit, and for understanding correctly the meaning of the creeds. (GCD, 25)

> From its earliest days the Church has recognized that liturgy and catechesis support each other. Prayer and the sacraments call for informed participants; fruitful participation in catechesis calls for the spiritual enrichment that comes from liturgical participation. . . .

> Sacramental catechesis has traditionally been of two kinds: preparation for the initial celebration of the sacraments and enrichment following their first reception. The first is elementary or general in

nature; it aims to introduce catechumens to the teaching of scripture and the creed. The second reflects on the meaning of the Christian mysteries and explores their consequences for Christian witness. Preparatory sacramental catechesis can be for a specified period of time — some weeks or months; the catechesis which follows is a lifetime matter. In the early church sacramental catechesis focused on the sacraments of initiation: baptism, confirmation and eucharist. (NCD, 36)

A PROCESS OF CONVERSION

Sacramental catechesis is first and foremost a process of conversion. It seeks to form people into a way of life, not just a way of knowing. It gradually invites people into the mystery (*sacramentum* in Greek) they will encounter in the celebration of the sacraments, the mystery revealed in the living word of God, in the symbols and gestures of the sacramental rites, and in the words and ritual prayers of those same sacramental rites. Sacramental catechesis invites people into the mystery of Christ, calling them into a sacramental sharing in his life, death and resurrection. The goal is the total transformation of the person, who begins to understand his or her own life in the context and in light of the paschal mystery of Jesus Christ.

CATECHESIS FROM AND TOWARD RITUAL

Sacramental formation flows from and toward the celebration of sacramental rites. The rite itself—including scripture, symbols, gestures, music and prayer texts—is the context for catechesis.

Sacramental catechesis includes formation in the word of God—the liturgy of the word. If the purpose of catechesis is to reveal the person of Jesus Christ, one place that mystery is revealed is in the proclamation of the scriptures, especially the gospel. The scriptures appointed for the sacramental rites are not just intended for proclamation; they also reveal the theology inherent in the sacramental experience. Thus, sacramental catechesis presumes formation in the word, which helps reveal the sacramental mystery.

Integral to this formation in the word is proclamation and preaching. The church teaches that Christ is present in the proclamation of the word in the midst of the celebrating assembly. Just as large, robust symbols are the best expression of the reality they embody, so too the presence of Christ in the word is most evident when the proclamation is worthy of the text it proclaims. When lectors and presiders proclaim the word of God with an informed understanding of the text and with prayerful, refined skill, their proclamation alone has the power to touch lives and transform hearts.

Preaching also has an important function in the celebration of the sacraments. Good sacramental preaching "enables the congregation to participate in the celebration with faith."[1] It invites the community into the sacramental mystery being celebrated and all the inherent symbols within that mystery—the scriptures, ritual action and sacramental symbols. Sacramental preaching (or any preaching for that matter) is not theological discourse. The "homily is preached in order that a community of believers who have gathered to celebrate the liturgy may do so more deeply and fully—more faithfully—and thus be formed for Christian witness in the world."[2] Preaching has as its end the same goal as the sacraments themselves—to form us for Christian witness in the world!

Sacramental catechesis assumes the participation of the faithful. Sacraments belong to all the faithful. They are not private. Thus, the locus for sacramental catechesis is the celebrating assembly. Within that assembly of believers, there are a variety of ministries to assist in the formation of those preparing for the sacraments, such as catechists, godparents, sponsors, clergy and musicians.

When sacraments are understood as belonging to the entire community and when the sacraments of initiation are a priority concern in the parish, everyone realizes that they have a role to play in the formation of people who are preparing for sacraments. Parishioners understand that their role is to be examples of Christian discipleship, to offer continued prayer support and encouragement to sacramental candidates, and to actively participate in the sacramental rites. Catechists are trained and prepared to assist those who are preparing for sacraments to enter into the sacramental mystery and to be transformed by the sacramental experience. Godparents and sponsors understand that they hold a sacred trust; as representative of the wider community they journey with their candidate. They apprentice them in the Christian life and in the life of the parish community. Musicians prepare the seasonal, Sunday and sacramental liturgies with a repertoire that supports the sacramental celebration. They are familiar with the sacramental rites and they know the role of music within those rites. The musician prepares music that invites active, conscious participation by those celebrating the sacraments as well as the entire assembly. The clergy remember that all ministry flows from its sacramental life and that sacraments are opportunities for ongoing conversion in the lives of all parishioners. With that in mind, their preaching, teaching and pastoral formation flows from and leads to the sacraments. The clergy understand their role as one of empowerment. They call forth, support and invite the ministry of all the baptized—ministry that extends beyond the parish borders—and they make sure that appropriate formation is provided for such ministry.

Finally, sacramental catechesis always assumes mystagogical reflection—catechesis that follows the celebration of the sacrament. This type of catechesis is required since one cannot really understand the sacramental encounter until one has experienced it.

Preparatory sacramental catechesis prepares candidates to fully and consciously encounter the sacramental symbols inherent in the celebration of the sacraments. Post-sacramental catechesis, also known as mystagogical catechesis, assists the candidates in recalling the sacramental symbols experienced in the sacrament—word, action, ritual prayer, symbol, gesture and music. Mystagogical catechesis invites candidates to remember their experience of the sacramental symbols and define them in light of their experience. It also assists them in appropriating meaning for their lives, which leads to their ongoing transformation. Mystagogical catechesis will be addressed in more detail in a later chapter.

SACRAMENTAL CATECHESIS AND THE *RITE OF CHRISTIAN INITIATION OF ADULTS*

The normative model of sacramental catechesis given to us by the church is the *Rite of Christian Initiation of Adults* (RCIA). This rite presents a vision of sacramental catechesis based in the practices of handing on the faith in the earliest centuries of the church and on the pioneering work of some catechists in the twentieth century. Prior to the promulgation of the RCIA (1972 in Latin, 1974 in English) such catechesis consisted primarily of doctrinal instruction. Preparation for entry into the Catholic church usually consisted of private classes or instructions. The parish priest met with an individual or small group to teach them the basic doctrines of the Catholic faith. Those preparing to join the church attended Mass anonymously; their baptism or reception into the church usually took place in a small, private ceremony.

The RCIA suggests a different model. It insists that initiation is the responsibility of all the baptized, including but not limited to the priest (RCIA, 9). It provides a model of formation that is incarnational, centered on the relationship of the individual with the person of Jesus Christ and with his body, the church. It centers catechesis in the primary place where that relationship is fostered and celebrated, in the community of faith that gathers Sunday by Sunday throughout the feasts and seasons of the liturgical year. "Within the cycle of the year the Church unfolds the whole mystery of Christ, from his incarnation and birth until his ascension, the day of Pentecost and the expectation of blessed hope and of the Lord's return" (Constitution on the Sacred Liturgy [CSL], 102). This model also respects the journey of each person. It assumes that those who come seeking initiation will be welcomed whenever they arrive, no matter what time of year that happens to be.

The goal of this liturgically centered model is to immerse new members in the life, death and resurrection of Jesus Christ and to have them continue his mission through his Holy Spirit. The doctrine that Saint Augustine insisted be indelibly imprinted on the heart of every candidate for initiation consisted of an explanation of the Nicene Creed, the Lord's Prayer, and the two great commandments: love of God and love of neighbor. He insisted that "what we are to believe, what we are to hope for, and what we are to love, is the sum total of Christian doctrine." In a nutshell, faith is relationally based.

In this new model of sacramental catechesis, the church uses the language of journey, conversion, discipleship and relationship. Rather than a program of specific instruction, the RCIA suggests a fluid, gradual process of formation, the heart of which is paschal mystery of Jesus Christ (RCIA, 8). The underlying assumption of the previous model of sacramental preparation was that education was required to understand the sacramental mysteries. In contrast, the RCIA, drawing from the mystagogical homilies of the early church, including those of Cyril of Jerusalem and Ambrose of Milan, insists that experience gives birth to meaning. Sacramental experience is followed by mystagogical reflection on that experience:

> A suitable catechesis is to be provided by priests or
> deacons, or by catechists and others of the faithful,
> planned to be gradual and complete in its coverage,

accommodated to the liturgical year and solidly supported by celebrations of the word. This catechesis
leads the catechumens not only to an appropriate
acquaintance with dogmas and precepts but also to a
profound sense of the mystery of salvation in which
they desire to participate. (RCIA, 75.1)

DOCTRINE

One criticism made of the type of sacramental catechesis that the
RCIA presents is that it is anti-doctrine. It is not. The rite affirms
that the handing on of doctrine is essential. It is the concern of every
adult member of the Christian community. However, doctrine is not
the only concern of the initiation process. The church presents us
with a broad vision of catechesis. In it, people are led into a life of
prayer, worship and action with the purpose of making committed,
apostolic disciples. "Since the Church's life is apostolic, catechumens
should learn how to work actively with others to spread the Gospel
and build up the Church by the witness of their lives and by profess-
ing their faith" (RCIA, 75.4).

While the former model no doubt expected a similar outcome,
our practice suggested that the way to achieve that goal was by making educated Catholics. The liturgical model embodied in the RCIA
assumes that the candidate is willing to enter into a process of deep
and lasting conversion to Jesus Christ:

The newly converted set out on a spiritual journey.
Already sharing through faith in the mystery of
Christ's death and resurrection, they pass from the
old to a new nature made perfect in Christ. Since this
transition brings with it a progressive change of outlook and conduct, it should become manifest by

means of social consequences and should develop gradually. (RCIA, 75.4)

The sacramental catechesis of the RCIA is situated in the liturgy itself. It understands that the liturgy is formative. Liturgy immerses the faithful in the life and mission of Christ. Liturgy remembers and makes present our encounter with the risen Christ, and it helps express an understanding of that encounter. "By means of sacred rites celebrated at successive times they are led into the life of faith, worship and charity belonging to the people of God" (RCIA, 76).

> Christ is always present in his Church, especially in
> its liturgical celebrations. . . .
>
> Every liturgical celebration, because it is an action
> of Christ the Priest and of his Body which is the
> Church, is a sacred action surpassing all others. . . .
> Liturgy is the source and summit toward which the
> activity of the Church is directed and the font from
> which her power flows. (CSL, 7, 10)

The RCIA does insist that preparation for initiation must include a "suitable catechesis" (RCIA, 75.1). The church teaches that the goal of catechesis is to reveal the person of Jesus Christ; since the gospel is the "principle witness of his life and teaching" (NCD, 60a, i), what better place than the Sunday liturgy, where the gospel is proclaimed and preached in the midst of the assembly of believers, to experience the type of catechesis called for in the RCIA?

If liturgy is the privileged home of catechesis, as the *Catechism of the Catholic Church* says (1074), then the liturgical year (RCIA, 75.1), not the nine-month school calendar, provides the appropriate schedule for this process. It is for this reason that the RCIA and the National Statutes insist that this is a gradual process, several years in duration if necessary, and that the catechumenate proper is to last at least one complete liturgical cycle (NS, 6).

NOTES

1. *"Fulfilled in Your Hearing: The Homily in the Sunday Assembly,"* The Bishops Committee on Priestly Life and Ministry, National Conference of Catholic Bishops, 1982, 17.

2. Ibid, 18.

CHAPTER 3

An Overview of the Periods and Rites of Initiation

When planning a road trip the traveler studies a map and considers the overall journey before mapping out the actual route. It is similarly important for initiation ministers to understand the overall vision of the *Rite of Christian Initiation of Adults* as they embark on the journey through its component parts. The first step in understanding the paradigm shift required to make the move to a year-round catechumenate is to consider the overarching principles inherent in each of the periods of the RCIA. Thus, this chapter will examine those principles and with broad strokes paint an overview of each of the periods of process.

THE PERIOD OF EVANGELIZATION, OR PRECATECHUMENATE

As we mentioned in the previous chapter, one of the assumptions of the *Rite of Christian Initiation of Adults* is that the unique journey of each individual is respected and accommodated. Thus, when uncatechized inquirers arrive, whether in February, June or September, they are welcomed and begin their period of precatechumenate. The length and season of this period of the catechumenal process is not defined; there is no official starting or ending date. An inquirer remains in the precatechumenate until he or she is evangelized and ready to declare publicly his or her intention to become a fully initiated member of the Catholic Christian community. This declaration and readiness is marked by the celebration of a liturgical rite.

RITES OF ACCEPTANCE AND WELCOME

For those who are unbaptized, the Rite of Acceptance into the Order of Catechumens is celebrated. For those who are uncatechized but baptized, the Rite of Welcoming the Candidates is celebrated. These rites are similar, but different enough that the dignity of the baptism already received is respected. These rites serve as the inquirers' ritual passageway into the next period of the process, called the period of the catechumenate. The Rites of Acceptance and/or Welcome are celebrated whenever someone is ready to move to the next stage of the process. Paragraph 18 in the RCIA suggests that they might be celebrated two or three times a year if necessary. What this presupposes is a catechumenal process that ministers to the needs of the people it serves and respects the conversion that is taking place in their lives. Only in an idealized world is every person evangelized according to a predetermined timetable. God's work in a human life is often messy and is not a respecter of our calendar. Thus, when the question is asked, How long will the precatechumenate period last and when does a person celebrate the Rite of Acceptance? the answer is, As long as it takes and whenever he or she is ready.

THE PERIOD OF THE CATECHUMENATE

The second period of the initiation process is called the period of the catechumenate. The RCIA is very explicit in determining the length of time spent in the catechumenate, although the date of the starting point is undefined: "The period of catechumenate, beginning at acceptance into the order of catechumens and including both the catechumenate proper and the period of purification and enlightenment after election or enrollment of names, should extend for at least one year of formation, instruction, and probation" (National Statutes, 6). The catechumenate lasts for at least one complete liturgical cycle (one full year) for uncatechized, unbaptized person as well as for those who are uncatechized but baptized. Why? In one full liturgical year, the church proclaims and celebrates the entire mystery of Christ. Persons seeking initiation are being incorporated into that mystery and into the community that celebrates and proclaims that mystery. Thus their primary formation in the paschal mystery of Christ takes place as it is celebrated and revealed in one complete liturgical cycle. The formation that flows from the liturgical cycle is gradual and complete, and it encompasses the four major dimensions of the church's life: word (both scripture and tradition), worship, mission and community (RCIA, 75).

The criteria for discerning when a baptized person who is somewhat catechized is to be received into the full communion of the Catholic church depend on the degree to which that person is catechized. Thus, that person's time in the catechumenate proper depends on his or her readiness to come into full communion. When it is discerned that the person is sufficiently catechized in the areas of catechesis defined by Catholic tradition (which we will explore in later chapters), the church celebrates the Rite of Reception into the Full Communion of the Catholic Church. The rite of reception may be celebrated more than once a year and at any time in the liturgical year, whenever someone is ready to complete the sacraments of initiation. Baptized, catechized persons from other ecclesial traditions do not necessarily belong in the catechumenate, but should be given a brief period of formation in the Catholic tradition in preparation for the completion of the sacraments of initiation (NS, 30).

THE RITE OF ELECTION AND THE CALL
TO CONTINUING CONVERSION

An unbaptized person who has been in the catechumenate for a year or longer and is discerned to be ready for initiation at the Easter Vigil participates in the Rite of Election, the liturgical rite that marks their entry into the next stage of the initiation process. A baptized person who has gone through the catechumenal process and who will celebrate the rite of reception at the Easter Vigil or during the Easter season may participate in a similar celebration, the Rite of Calling the Candidates to Continuing Conversion. This catapults them into the next period of formation and spiritual preparation, the period of purification and enlightenment, which usually coincides with Lent.

PERIOD OF PURIFICATION AND ENLIGHTENMENT

The period of purification and enlightenment prepares the elect and candidates for the celebration of the sacraments of baptism, confirmation and eucharist at the Easter Vigil. During this lenten time of spiritual preparation the elect prepare for and celebrate the penitential rites called scrutinies. The baptized candidates prepare for and celebrate a similar penitential rite and participate in the sacrament of reconciliation. The faithful support and pray for the elect and candidates as they engage in final preparation for the Easter sacraments. At the same time, the faithful, too, prepare to renew their baptismal promises at Easter.

THE SACRAMENTS OF INITIATION AND
THE PERIOD OF MYSTAGOGY

When the sacraments of initiation—baptism, confirmation and eucharist—have been celebrated, the newly baptized (called neophytes) and the newly received enter into the period of mystagogy (from the Greek, meaning to uncover or lead into the mystery). Like the period of the catechumenate, the heart of the period of mystagogy is the Sunday eucharist. The neophytes and the newly received spend the Easter season reflecting on the paschal mystery, the gospel, the sacramental mysteries they have celebrated and what it means to "become the bread they have received" out in the world. When the Easter season ends, they continue to gather monthly for renewal and further reflection on the gospel until the next Easter. Like the periods of precatechumenate and catechumenate, the period of mystagogy is fluid and open-ended. People entering into full communion throughout the year participate in mystagogical reflection following their celebration of the initiation sacraments.

POSTSCRIPT

For some ministers of initiation, the vision presented here and in the previous chapter represents a very different way of thinking about, understanding and practicing Christian initiation. Making such changes requires a huge commitment. If we are to undertake these changes, we must ask, What theology informs what we want to change? and What vision are we trying to adhere to? If we do not answer these questions, we may end up changing nothing but our schedules. We risk doing for twelve months what we had been accomplishing in nine. If we do not ground our practice in the vision and theology of the rite, any change is futile.

CHAPTER 4

The Initiating Community

The primary locus of initiation is the community of believers. This chapter will reflect on exactly what that means. What does it mean to be an initiating community?

For years the term *initiating community* has been floating through initiation circles and many of us wonder, What is an initiating community, anyway? Does my parish qualify? If not, how might we get qualified? The *Rite of Christian Initiation of Adults* tells us that the responsibility of initiation belongs to all the baptized (RCIA, 9). Christian initiation assumes a vibrant, initiating community. Does that mean that we should suspend our RCIA teams, fire our catechists and then one Sunday stand proudly before our assemblies and announce to everyone that the job of initiation is now being handed over to every one of them—good luck and Godspeed? Imagine how that would go over!

For those of us already facing the many challenges of ministry in our parishes, the concept of an initiating community only adds to our frustration. The truth is that such a community is not far from our grasp. Perhaps we are members of such a community but simply do not recognize it.

WHAT ATTRACTS NEW MEMBERS?

The church exists to regenerate itself by constantly bringing people into the unity of Christ. Thus the church must always be attracting people to itself. Why do people continue to knock on our doors? Yes, God is calling them, but there are many places vying for the opportunity to respond to that call. Why the Catholic church? Why one particular parish? What is it about your community that attracts people to "come and see"? Of the many things that might attract people, two elements seem to be most frequently cited by those who have come to us: the people and the liturgy.

The People

More often than not, people knock on our door because of the influence of other Christians. One man was so touched by the way in which a Christian community reached out to his dying father that he decided it was time to seek the living Christ in his own life. The witness of other Christians—the way they live the gospel and reach out to the poor, the sick and suffering, and to neighbors in distress—is a primary indication of whether or not a parish has within it the seeds of initiation.

People who live the gospel of Christ have much to teach us about what it means to be an initiating, welcoming community, even if our parishes have a long way to go before they would be classified as such! What is it about such people that makes Christianity so attractive to others? Historians insist that one important factor responsible for the spread of Christianity in the ancient world was *agápe*—"See how they love one another." The love and concern that members of the community extended to each other attracted people, especially in a culture that did not value such behavior.

Love, care and hospitality are still characteristics by which one might identify a true minister of the gospel. Ministers of the gospel offer the compassion of Christ to others. Who are those people in our communities? They are often too busy to be on our "initiation teams." They are not, however, too busy to share the message of God's love with other human beings. There word *team* does not appear in the RCIA; there are ministries, and the primary minister of

Christian initiation is "all the baptized" (RCIA, 9). Thus, the saints in the pews indeed are, de facto, full-fledged members of our "initiation teams."

If initiation belongs to all the baptized, then why not invite the living saints within our communities to come and share their love and their lives with our catechumenal groups? When trying to share the healing face of Christ, why not invite a parishioner who is imbued with Christ's compassion, one who consistently reaches out to the sick and suffering, to come and share his or her story with those preparing for sacramental initiation? Further, why not ask that living saint to take a candidate for initiation with him or her on the next apostolic mission?

Sometimes our programmatic mindsets keep us from understanding that initiatory catechesis is rooted in the Catholic Christian life of ordinary (and sometimes not so ordinary) parishioners. We bemoan our frustration at trying to get people to assume their baptismal responsibility, yet we fail to see the resources right under our noses. Perhaps what is lacking is the imagination needed to tap even the most sedate parish communities. Welcoming, initiating ministers of God's love exist in even the driest, most inhospitable parishes. We need to seek them out and find creative ways to allow them to do what they do best: share the good news through the witness of their lives. Perhaps it is as simple as asking them to invite an inquirer or catechumen to come to their home for dinner (RCIA, 9.1) or to accompany them as they live the corporal and spiritual works of mercy.

The Liturgy

The Sunday liturgy is the second major element of attraction that people report. Many folks come to us because they have experienced the presence of God in the sacrament of community, word and eucharist when attending Mass, perhaps on a specific occasion, or more regularly, with a spouse or friend. Something about Catholic liturgy was inviting to them.

This would seem to indicate that one place to begin in implementing or improving the process of initiation is the Sunday liturgy. People are attracted to our incarnational, sacramental way of life. Does the community's liturgy reflect a lively, vibrant faith? Are the symbols strong and robust? Is the community welcoming and hospitable? How are strangers and outsiders welcomed (or not) on a regular basis? Is there enthusiastic participation by the assembly? Does the community take ownership of the liturgy, or is it understood only as the priest's concern? Does the music reflect praise, thanks and worship of God, as well as a call to mission, service and care for the weakest members of society? Does the liturgy invite mission and discipleship? How is that reflected in the life of the parish community? When any of those things are lacking, they need our serious attention.

Another important element in a liturgy that attracts people into the community is that it includes those already in the community as active participants, highlighting their baptismal role and responsibility. An initiating community prays the rites of the catechumenal process with those journeying through the initiation process. A parish where the assembly is largely reduced to the role of spectator on an ordinary Sunday will be much the same when initiation rites are celebrated. Liturgy is the place where the primary formation of catechumens and candidates takes place, so it had better reflect and celebrate what is intended. Does it?

Every parish community has the seeds of initiation within it. Those seeds may be no larger than the smallest mustard seed, but we know to what proportion they can grow! Initiation ministers need to look for ways to foster and nourish the initiating gifts already present in every community to blossom.

CHAPTER 5

The Period of Evangelization: Precatechumenate

The language that the church uses for the first period in the initiation process lays out the path for the entire initiation process for adults and children of catechetical age. The first period of the Rite of Christian Initiation of Adults is called the period of evangelization. The title itself tells us what is to take place during this period: evangelization. But what does the church mean by evangelization?

In *Evangelii Nuntiandi*, Paul VI gave us a clear vision of evangelization. Pope Paul insisted that evangelization involves bringing the basic Christian message of salvation, the good news, to the whole world. At the heart of this message is the love of Jesus, which comes to us by the grace of God. Evangelization is meant not just to encompass our religious lives, but also to reach to all areas of society. Its purpose is to transform human beings, to bring about a deep interior transformation and conversion of individuals and the entire world. Evangelization, insists Paul VI, includes the evangelization of culture, reaching into our homes, our schools, our marketplaces, our politics and the world. It is the essential mission of the church: "The Church exists to evangelize" (*Evangelii Nuntiandi*, 14).

Further, evangelization is the responsibility of all the baptized. "Evangelization in all its dimensions needs to be at the core of parish identity as it is the essential mission of the whole church."[1] All Christians, all parish members, are to witness and profess the marvels of God both by word and example. Pope Paul insisted that we must be more intentional in our efforts. Evangelization is a priority.

Evangelization has been a constant theme and focus during Pope John Paul II's pontificate. The new *General Directory for Catechesis* (1997) emphasizes the importance of evangelization by shifting our understanding of catechesis. Prior to this document, catechesis was situated in the church's ministry of the word. Catechesis is now situated within the ministry of evangelization. That means that all of the church's catechetical efforts now are directed toward spreading the message of God's love in the world and in bringing about the transformation of human beings.

The church insists that all catechetical efforts spring from an initiatory, evangelization model. What that means is that the heart of all of our efforts to pass on the faith is metanoia—deep, personal, intentional conversion to Christ evidenced by a life lived in conformity with the gospel.

Therefore, when the *Rite of Christian Initiation of Adults* names the first period of the initiation process the period of evangelization, the content of this period is made clear: "Faithfully and constantly the living God is proclaimed and Jesus Christ whom he has sent for the salvation of all" (RCIA, 36). This evangelization calls for initial conversion. It prompts conversion and invites inquirers to turn away from sin—a transformation of the entire person.

WHO BELONGS IN THE PRECATECHUMENATE?

If the purpose of the precatechumenate is evangelization, then only those people who need to be evangelized belong in this period. What does it mean to be evangelized? Paragraph 42 of the RCIA sets forth the discernment criteria for those unbaptized and baptized candidates who are ready to move to the period of the catechumenate by celebrating a Rite of Acceptance or a Rite of Welcome:

The prerequisite for making this first step [the Rite of Acceptance] is that the beginnings of the spiritual life and the fundamentals of Christian teaching have taken root in the candidates. Thus there must be evidence of the first faith that was conceived during the period or evangelization and precatechumenate and of an initial conversion and intention to change their lives and to enter into a relationship with God in Christ. Consequently, there must also be evidence of the first stirrings of repentance, a start to the practice of the company and spirit of Christians through contact with a priest or with members of the community. The candidates should also be instructed about the celebration of the liturgical Rite of Acceptance.

The period of the precatechumenate for any particular individual should be long enough for the person to develop according to these principles. If someone meets these criteria when he or she enters our processes of initiation, a period of evangelization may not be necessary. Some individuals may meet some, but not all, the criteria. Thus, a person may enjoy an intimate relationship with Jesus Christ, understand the principles of Christian teaching, have begun the practice of prayer, have a familiarity with the great stories of the Bible and be aware of their need for repentance, yet have no sense whatsoever of the church. This person would need time to develop a familiarity with the church, the community and individuals within the church. He or she would need sufficient time to become aware of the desire to become a Catholic.

Who belongs in the precatechumenate? People who are:

1) uncatechized (read—un-evangelized) and unbaptized.

2) uncatechized and baptized.

3) uncatechized, baptized Catholics who have yet to complete their initiation.

The length of time a person spends in the precatechumenate depends on the extent to which the individual has been evangelized, as determined by the criterion set forth in the rite. The next chapter deals more deeply with issues concerning baptized candidates.

STORYTELLING

The primary vehicle for accomplishing the goals of the precatechumenate period is storytelling. The Good News of Jesus Christ is the greatest story ever told, but it cannot be spread unless someone tells it. The main focus of the period of evangelization is to share that story. Famed Rabbi Abraham Heschel maintains that there are no proofs for the existence of God, there are only witnesses. During this period, the ministers of initiation have the task of not only telling the stories, but also helping each inquirer connect those stories to his or her own story of faith. They also witness to the power and action of God in their own lives and in the life of the community.

CONVERSION

As already stated, the purpose of this period is to help inquirers get in touch with the action of God in their lives and enter into a deep, abiding and personal relationship with Christ. The primary purpose of this period is not to teach Catholic doctrine or practices, but to facilitate the conversion of the inquirers. The heart of that conversion is the gospel of Jesus Christ—his life, passion, death, resurrection and sending of the Spirit as it unfolds in the various accounts in the gospels. Especially meaningful are the stories that reveal who Jesus is and the stories that invite us into relationship with him. The core stories of the Old Testament are also brought to bear on the conversion of heart and mind. What better way to encounter the love God has for all creation than to remember the primal stories and themes of the Old Testament—creation, exodus, God's covenant with humanity, and the power and presence of God in the community.

If conversion is not central to the initiation process, it becomes a "head trip," a solely intellectual process that works well in making informed Catholics, but poorly in making committed disciples. That does not mean, however, that specific questions about Catholic faith and practices are not asked. People come with their questions, and it is the responsibility of the catechist to answer those questions, even to raise a few.

CONTENT

The RCIA sets forth the agenda for the precatechumenate period. Stories of scripture and the stories of faith that invite the inquirer to embark on a journey of conversion to Christ become primary issues in this period (RCIA, 36, 37). Transformation of behavior and attitudes is the benchmark by which one discerns whether or not this conversion is taking place. The RCIA reminds us that the inquirer begins to "feel called away from sin and into the mystery of God's love" (#37). The text further shows us the agenda of this period by telling us what the discernment criteria are for a person to move into the next period of the process (#42). These are the issues of primary concern, and therefore the "content" of the precatechumenate:

1) Beginning of the spiritual life

2) Fundamentals of Christian teaching

3) Evidence of first faith

4) Initial conversion

5) Intention to change one's life

6) Intention to enter into deep relationship with God in Christ

7) First stirring of repentance

8) Calling on God in prayer

9) Sense of the church

10) Experience of community.

Those who are inquiring determine the agenda. Formation is based on the needs of the inquirers rather than on a predefined agenda. Catechists need to be prepared to lead precatechumenate sessions, which requires that they prepare material with a particular focus, but they must also be ready to change plans and adapt to the needs of the inquirers.

For example, one catechist tells how she was prepared to lead the inquirers in a session about what it means to be part of a faith community (sense of the Church, #42). An inquirer asked what seemed to be an unrelated question. She wanted to talk about God's forgiveness. The question derailed the catechist's plan. The inquirer became extremely agitated. When she composed herself, she told the group that the biggest obstruction in continuing to pursue her dream to become Catholic was the sacrament of reconciliation. She had heard some very frightening things about the sacrament. Her primary fear was telling another human being the terrible things she had done in her life. She felt they were beyond God's forgiveness and redemption. The wise catechist gently took her by the hand and told her that there is no sin so terrible that it is beyond the power of God's love and forgiveness. She told the inquirer that the sacrament of reconciliation is a way for us to touch the healing, reconciling presence of God in our lives. It is a way for us to experience the embrace of God who loves us unconditionally, like a mother loves her precious child.

The woman wept and her fear melted away. Had the catechist been insistent on carrying out her planned agenda, the group would have missed that healing epiphany. Everyone in the room was touched by the experience.

Inquirers may have a fairly good sense of the fundamentals of the Christian way of life, but little sense of the need to enter into a process of conversion and transformation. In such a case, more time is needed for sharing stories that invite conversion and repentance.

During this period of evangelization inquirers are invited to look at their lives and conform their daily living to gospel values. They are introduced to a loving and forgiving God and are subsequently invited to see the need for repentance in their lives.

The precatechumenate period is a time for growing in the practice of calling on God in prayer. Inquirers are invited to enter into intimate relationship with God and are shown ways to grow in that relationship. Catechists help the inquirers discover the conscious and unconscious ways they have prayed throughout their lives. Inquirers learn that their casual conversation with God is indeed prayer, and they are encouraged to develop that conversation further. They are reminded that intimate relationships require intimate conversation, but they also require active listening. Thus, the inquirer is invited to spend time listening for God to speak to their hearts and to discern God's action in their lives. The inquirer is reminded that there are many different ways to call on God in prayer and are introduced to a broad array of prayer experiences. They can pray formal prayers from the Christian tradition such as the Acts of Faith, Hope and Charity or other prayers such as litanies and acclamations. Inquirers are also reminded that they need look no further than the book of Psalms for the greatest prayer book ever crafted. They are invited to begin the practice of praying the psalms as a regular habit of prayer throughout their lives. The period of the precatechumenate, therefore, is a time for inquirers to taste the various models of prayer, thereby beginning the Christian discipline of prayer that will remain with them for the rest of their lives.

The period of the precatechumenate is also a time to become familiar with the church community. The RCIA suggests that inquirers be invited into the home of parishioners, recognizing the role of the entire parish (RCIA, 9) in this process of evangelization. Thus, inquirers are to be encouraged to get involved in the life of the parish and to begin to forge friendships within the parish community. Parishioners need to be reminded that there are people inquiring into the Catholic way of life in the parish. Parishioners should then be encouraged to seek them out, perhaps inviting them to their homes for a meal. Perhaps members of the community might be invited to gather with inquirers to support them in faith and to share their own stories of God's action in their lives. The precatechumenate begins the process of incorporating them into parish life.

If the precatechumenate is a time to begin the process of incorporating the inquirer into the life of the community, what better way to accomplish that than inviting and escorting them to parish social activities? For example, our parish likes to gather for parish picnics. Formal precatechumenate sessions are suspended on those days, and everyone participates in the picnic. The inquirers are then escorted around the picnic grounds and introduced to parishioners. It is a wonderful way to make connections—young mothers connect with other young mothers, young married couples with others, for example. One elderly inquirer made a connection with a member of our elderly community club, which meets for social activities. She became involved in that organization and later shared how quickly she acclimated to parish life as a result of her participation in that group. Creative initiation ministers should constantly find ways to help the inquirers make those important parish connections.

It is also a time to reflect on the paschal mystery and the paschal nature (RCIA, 8) of the Christian journey. The first public ritual celebrated by the inquirers, the Rite of Acceptance, is the first public declaration of their intent to join the church. In this rite, inquirers are signed with the cross of Jesus Christ. How can we ask them to do that unless we have shared what it means to live the cross in our everyday lives? Thus, another purpose of this period of evangelization is to prepare people for a lifetime of living the paschal mystery. From the very beginning, the period of evangelization sets out to help people enter into and participate in that mystery. Each baptized person enters the waters of death and resurrection and is born to new life in Christ. This mystery is lived out in our daily lives every time we join our suffering, sorrow and joy—our very lives to the suffering and sacrifice of Christ. When we join our lives to Christ's paschal mystery, we not only offer ourselves to God, but we offer our lives for the sake of others. We participate in Christ's own work of redemption—our lives, too, are offered for the salvation of the world. Every time someone reaches out to another suffering soul or shares his or her own pain to alleviate that of others, that person shares in the work of Christ on the cross. When we live the paschal mystery, we are given the opportunity to discover incredible meaning for our lives—we are able to find meaning in the midst of life's struggles as well as life's joys.

One of the most exciting realities in the church today is that the model for all ministry is the initiation process. What we do with inquirers and catechumens should be the benchmark for what we do in all formation in the church today. Since evangelization is the primary mission of the church, more attention than ever before is given to the abiding conversion of its members. That is truly good news.

PORTRAIT OF A CANDIDATE

Maureen has just arrived at our doorstep. What brings her to us? The Maureens who knock on our doors bring with them varied and diverse experiences—conscious and unconscious—of God's action in their lives. They are seekers responding to God's gratuitous, grace-filled invitation. That invitation takes many forms. Perhaps Maureen was touched by a loving disciple of the Lord and desires to know more about the peace and joy she observed in that individual. Perhaps her life is surrounded by chaos and struggle, and in the midst of the confusion she is seeking to find meaning for her life. Thus, she turns to the church that offered great consolation to a friend who was in crisis. Perhaps Maureen is engaged to a fine, young Catholic man and wants to share his faith. Perhaps Maureen knew for a long time that she needed a church home, but was reticent to make the first step. Or is it possible that Maureen simply experienced an awareness of God's love in her life and now desires to grow in that intimate union?

HOSPITALITY

What should be our response to Maureen? Our first response is to offer divine hospitality. We have much to learn from our ancestors in the faith. Ancient cultures believed that offering hospitality, especially to strangers, was a religious act, a sacred responsibility. To refuse to extend hospitality was considered a sacrilege. The nomadic Israelites knew well what it meant to be a stranger in a foreign land. The extension of hospitality to another human being was the same as offering God's love and mercy to that person. Divine hospitality was a common metaphor for God's protection and care for Israel. In the New Testament Christ became the object of that hospitality. To welcome anyone in the name of Jesus was the same as offering the gift of Jesus to that person. Offering Christ's hospitality to others is a sign that the reign of God is indeed in our midst. It is a witness to God's love.

Thus, we must approach inquirers ready to offer Christ's love, compassion, hospitality and understanding. We are ambassadors for Christ. As ministers we are responsible for gently leading people into an intimate encounter with Jesus Christ. Most of the time folks come to us with an infant faith. Some of the time they are aware of God's presence in their lives and they desire to grow in that relationship within the Catholic tradition. Sometimes they know about God, but have yet to experience God's presence on a conscious level. Sometimes other circumstances and agendas drive their need to inquire. Our responsibility is to walk with them and lead them more deeply into the sacred encounter with Christ. One way we pass on the Catholic expression of that encounter is by living it and inviting the inquirers to live it with us.

If we were to invite strangers into our home, what would we do? We would make them feel welcome, we would ask about their lives and then we would tell them about ours. We would show them around and make them feel comfortable in our home. We would tell stories of our family that would help the stranger get to know us in ways that went beyond the formalities of name and vital statistics. In turn, we would seek to know the stranger in a similar fashion.

If we were to entertain overnight guests in our home we would certainly lead them on a tour of our surroundings once they arrived. We would show them their sleeping quarters, the restroom facilities and the place for meals. We might even point out objects in the home that carry special significance for the family. Perhaps during the meal we would mention Aunt Sophie's heirloom silverware that we were using, and talk about our memories of our last meal with her.

Inquirers are entering a journey leading them to full membership in our Christian Catholic family. It is important that they become familiar with the parish family's surroundings. Thus, very early in their initiation journey, it is important to show inquirers around the parish and give them the opportunity to become familiar with the surroundings, the church appointments and the parish history. The best person to lead such a tour is not necessarily the initiation minister. If initiation belongs to all the baptized (RCIA, 9), perhaps the persons best equipped to show new inquirers around the parish are those who have been in the parish for many years. Who but they know the parish stories, its milestone events and its history?

How are hospitality and welcoming embodied in our relationship with inquirers? The first way is through storytelling. Before they ever enter a formal session in the parish, storytelling begins and sets the stage for a lifetime of storytelling. The ministers' role is to empower and invite inquirers to share the story of their lives, by asking who they are, what is their family experience, and what is their life's vocation?

DISCERNMENT

We also ask inquirers what brings them to this place and what it is they seek. These are key questions. Because inquirers will be asked to answer them at the Rite of Acceptance, when they make their first public commitment to become a Catholic Christian, we had better address these questions early and keep addressing them throughout the initial formation period.

What do you seek? In what way are you aware of God's presence or action in your life? Inquirers are invited to express to others—perhaps to name out loud for the first time—God's action in their lives. This is initial discernment, the first in an ongoing process of discernment. Our attention must turn to the *Rite of Christian Initiation of Adults* for a guide in knowing the questions that we must continue asking in order to best serve the needs of those who come to us.

The RCIA tells us how to discern to what extent a person is evangelized. The RCIA insists that there are observable criteria that help us discern the readiness of an individual to take the first ritual step toward initiation. From the first day of encounter, our role as ministers of initiation is to lead inquirers into a deep and abiding relationship with Jesus Christ and the gospel he came to proclaim (RCIA, 36). We need to invite them to open their hearts and their eyes to the action of the Holy Spirit in their lives (#36). We need to lead them through the stories of our lives and theirs, through the great stories of scripture and the grace of God into metanoia. Seeds of lasting conversion need to begin to take root in the life of the inquirer (#37). The inquirer needs to grow in his or her awareness of the sin in their lives as well as an awareness of God's love and mercy (#37). The inquirer needs to grow in the practice of prayer, to have a budding sense of the church and be aware of the need for Christian community (#42). The issues for discernment are the same issues used to determine the "content" of the evangelization of this period, embodied in paragraph 36 and following.

The issues of readiness embodied in paragraph 42 help determine the questions we need to pose and continue to raise. Does this person have a personal relationship with Jesus Christ? "Maureen, do you pray? How do you pray? Do you have an awareness of the presence of Jesus/God in your life? Do you read the Bible? What has it meant to you? Have you ever been part of a faith community? If you do enjoy an intimate relationship with Jesus, have you grown in your awareness of the sin in your life and your need for his forgiveness? Have you noticed a change in your life as a result of your relationship with Christ?" These and similar questions help the ministers of initiation become aware of the action of God in the inquirer's life: to know to what extent this person has been evangelized.

Recently, a man came to us seeking full initiation in the Catholic church. He was baptized in a Protestant church as an infant, but had not been part of a faith community since he was a very young child. There was a divorce in his family, and his participation in church came to a halt by the time he was seven years old. One might be tempted to assume that the gentleman would need a prolonged period of evangelization. After asking the appropriate questions, however, we learned that the man had a lifetime relationship with the Lord. He had come from a long line of preachers. While the man was not part of a faith community, there were people who shared the word and were models of faith for him as he grew into adulthood. The man lived in continuous communication with the Lord. When asked if he prayed, he responded by saying that he did not think he did. However, after he answered several questions about his relationship with Jesus, it became obvious that not only did he pray, but his prayer was part of the fabric of his life; it was intimate, ongoing dialogue with the Jesus he knew very well. He simply never termed his relationship "prayer." Even though he knew a few stories from the Bible, he had not ever formally read it. In some ways this man was evangelized; he knows Jesus. He had a sense of his own sinfulness and knew that he needed to continue to change. What was completely undeveloped, however, was a sense of the church (#42). He had not been part of a church since he was a small child. The impetus for becoming Catholic was a desire to share the church of his beloved wife and his dearest friend. This inquirer had little awareness of what it means to be part of a Christian community. He would be in the period of evangelization for a shorter period of time, however, than someone who was still operating out of an unconscious relationship with Christ. Appropriate, sensitive questions and the discerning grace of God helped the catechists walk with this man and lead him in his journey of faith.

If we allow the questions and answers to surface, the inquirers will tell us what we need to know to serve them in their initiation journey. Perhaps the inquirer only recently experienced God and never before had any contact with a Christian community. That person will obviously need an extended period of evangelization.

In contrast, perhaps the person has been living an ongoing, committed Christian life in another ecclesial tradition and now desires full communion of the Catholic church. That person certainly does not need to be evangelized; he or she is already living a committed life of discipleship. That person might simply need a process of sacramental preparation that highlights our ecclesial differences and assists them in preparing for the sacraments.

People do not come to us in neatly wrapped packages. Life is messy, and very often that messiness is the catalyst that brings people knocking in the first place. Our encounters with inquirers must be free of judgments on their past failures. All traces of triumphalism are to be expelled from our consciousness. Attitudes such as, "Well, sister, you have come to the right and the only place! You are finally on the right track!" have no place in our relationship with inquirers. It would be abuse to suggest to inquirers that everything God has previously accomplished in their lives is null and void now that they have stumbled on the truth.

While we seldom overtly demonstrate such an attitude, it often appears in subtle forms. One possible way this rears its head is by passing out literature containing testimonials from other seekers,

Protestant mostly, who have turned away from their former churches and have now embraced the "real and only truth." Recently a sponsor shared how she had given a baptized candidate a book which emphatically pointed out the "error" of this woman's previous tradition. While this sponsor's action was well intentioned, it was hardly hospitable. Ecumenism demands that we avoid triumphal attitudes (National Statutes, 33).

While it would not be advisable to approach an inquirer about past marital failures during a first meeting, it is nevertheless important that marital status of the inquirer (and his or her spouse) be determined early in the process. If an annulment is needed, the sooner that process gets underway, the better.

It is important for someone in the initiation ministry to have enough knowledge about annulments to help guide the inquirer in taking the appropriate steps to begin the annulment process. Thus, it is important that the initiation minister know what situations may require an annulment and to whom the inquirer should be referred to begin that process.

MINISTRIES

Who ministers to inquirers? The primary minister is the parish community. In its purest form the RCIA envisions a community that embraces inquirers and brings them to faith. Rural communities probably reflect the purest vision of the initiation process. Small, rural communities seldom have highly organized structures to minister to people seeking initiation. There are, however, people of faith who are willing to share that faith with those who seek initiation. This sharing can happen as informally as gathering with people around a kitchen table, in the parking lot or in people's living rooms.

Urban settings often require a more structured approach. Yet even within that structure there is room for great diversity and creativity. Some parishes enlist their small Christian communities in this important ministry of evangelization. In such instances the communities agree to minister to inquirers in the parish as part of their outreach. In other communities people agree to invite inquirers into their homes for a specified period of time to share faith with them and to walk with them during this time of conversion.

How does a parish maintain the necessary ministers to keep a year-round structure going week after week? How do catechists commit to minister week after week, year after year? They cannot; it is too much. Our vision needs to be expanded. Many parishes struggle with these questions.

A PARISH RESPONSE

People lead very busy lives, making it difficult for spiritual matters to compete with the many other demands on people's precious time. However, Sunday, the Lord's Day, is the day most people set aside for spiritual concerns. After asking inquirers what the most ideal time for them to meet would be, the catechists in my parish determined that Sunday would be the day. We discovered that families were busy with sports and other concerns every night of the week. The precatechumenate sessions were moved to Sunday morning. There were numerous advantages to such a move in our particular ministry setting. It would begin the habit of Sunday with inquirers. It would also be easier to enlist, keep and maintain initiation ministers, whose lives were just as busy as the lives of the inquirers, if they met on Sundays. This schema happened to be an effective pastoral adaptation in our parish setting. However, it might not be the best approach for every parish.

Burnout is a serious concern when ministers are asked to minister 52 weeks out of the year. Over the years we have repeatedly adapted as our needs changed. Thus, three sets of precatechumenate catechists were formed. Each of the three groups ministered in the precatechumenate for a specific period of time. Presently, each catechist group ministers for two months at a time with much flexibility built into their proposed schedule. The catechists meet monthly to keep abreast of what is happening in the lives of the people in the process.

PRECATECHUMENATE MINISTERS

The best precatechumenate ministers are storytellers. They know the great stories of scripture and can relate those stories to their own lives and the lives of others. These ministers must also practice the art of active listening. They need to know how to listen to the cues that signal opportunities for breakthrough, the "a-ha" moments. They must resist the temptation to teach didactically or to offer advice. Very often the best precatechumenate ministers are people who have led or have been part of faith-sharing groups and are proficient with the dynamics of Christian witness. Precatechumenate ministers must have etched in their memories the discernment criteria found in paragraph 42 so they might be always ready to seize the moment to lead the inquirers more deeply into the elements of conversion intended in this period. Precatechumenate catechists must also be willing to enter into honest, discerning dialogue with inquirers when it comes to readiness to move to the next period of the process.

READINESS FOR THE RITES OF ACCEPTANCE AND WELCOME

When does an inquirer celebrate the Rite of Acceptance or Welcome? The easiest answer is, When he or she is ready. Paragraph 18 suggests that two or three dates in a year should be set aside for this celebration.[2] What this suggests is that the period of evangelization is fluid and that people move through the process when it is discerned they are ready to move. Thus, the criteria set forth in the Rite of

Acceptance or Welcome (RCIA, 42) determine the people's readiness. When that readiness is achieved, the inquirer celebrates the rite.

However, the RCIA does suggest that the time for such a celebration should be delayed until a sufficient number of candidates are ready to proceed. Rigid adherence to paragraph 18—insistence that only two or three times be set aside for the celebration of the rite—may place undue restraint on the person who is ready to move into the next period. The spirit of that paragraph is that it recognizes that one, two or even three celebrations may not be sufficient. In our parish, for example, to celebrate only two or three Rites of Acceptance a year runs the risk of detaining a person in the precatechumenate unnecessarily for months at a time. Our parish rarely has more than eight people in the precatechumenate at any given time even though we fully initiate about thirty people throughout the year. Thus, one person might conceivably be ready to move to the period of the catechumenate when the other seven are relatively new to the process. It would be pastorally irresponsible to ask one person to remain in the precatechumenate until such time as the others are ready to celebrate the Rite of Acceptance or Welcome. The rule of thumb that works best in our pastoral situation is to celebrate a Rite of Acceptance or Welcome whenever someone is ready to celebrate it.

MAKING THE SHIFT

The logistics of moving to a continuous precatechumenate often seems overwhelming to someone wanting to make the shift. People continue to think in terms of their present practice. The best way to make the shift is to think in terms of doing something that may have no resemblance to one's experience. The following are key principles that are helpful to remember when making this shift.

No Fixed Beginning

There is no official, annual beginning date to the precatechumenate. Once the shift has been made, the precatechumenate simply continues *ad infinitum*—all year long, every year. People enter the precatechumenate as soon as they arrive on our doorstep—winter, spring, summer or fall. Thus, some people in the precatechumenate may be seasoned inquirers while others are brand new to the process.

No Fixed Ending

People leave the precatechumenate when they are ready to move—and not a moment sooner! When people are discerned to be ready to move into the period of the catechumenate, they celebrate the Rite of Acceptance or Welcome and proceed to the next period of the process accordingly.

For the Unevangelized

Those who are already evangelized according to the principles set forth in the rite (RCIA, 36–47) do not belong in the precatechumenate. They move directly into the catechumenate.

Informal and Adaptable

The precatechumenate is informal by nature. A classroom setting speaks volumes without uttering a word regarding the proposed agenda: The inquirers are there to "learn," and the catechist is there to "teach." An informal, casual setting, such as someone's home or a "living room" environment created in a parish building, helps create a space that invites sharing, storytelling and honest dialogue. Adapting to each parish's cultural or pastoral setting is crucial. It is important to get out of the program mode and think in terms of conversion and evangelization.

When the period of the catechumenate is as ongoing and fluid as the period of the precatechumenate, there is little reason to detain a person when he or she is ready to move to the next period of the process. However, it is wise to wait a few weeks if it is determined that other inquirers might be ready to celebrate the rite at that time. Good pastoral judgment should always be exercised in determining such things.

Requires Special Gifts in a Catechist

Catechists for the precatechumenate are not necessarily catechists in the catechumenate. Some people may or may not have the gifts to minister in both areas. For example, one woman in our parish was a catechist in the catechumenate. She realized that being a catechist in that forum was simply not her gift, and it caused her much stress. After talking with the initiation coordinator, she and the coordinator realized that she was far better suited to the dynamics of the precatechumenate. She loved to tell stories and to witness to God's action in her life and in the lives of others. She spent some time observing and participating in the precatechumenate and discovered that she had found her niche.

The Evangelized Become Evangelizers

One question that always surfaces is, Don't the inquirers tire of hearing the same stories of faith over and over? If new people continuously enter the process, isn't there, by necessity, a great deal of repetition? While this is a logical concern, it seldom becomes a problem unless the person expressing angst over the repetition is long overdue for moving into the next period. The beautiful dynamic that emerges in the process is that the seasoned inquirers become storytellers in their own right—they enter into the process of evangelization and witness to God's action in their own lives. They find new expressions of God's action in the events of their lives even when relating the same event on numerous occasions.

THE RITE OF ACCEPTANCE

Having been evangelized, our inquirer, Maureen, is ready to take the first ritual step on the journey toward becoming a fully initiated Catholic Christian. She has grown in her relationship with Jesus Christ. She has become aware of her sinfulness and has taken steps to change sinful behavior; she is aware of her need for forgiveness and reconciliation. She has noticed changes in her life and has begun to live her life in accord with biblical principles. She has begun to embrace a paschal way of life as she seeks to enter into the cycle of death and resurrection in her everyday life. She has reflected on the meaning of suffering in her life and prays for the strength to join her suffering to the suffering of Christ, thus participating in his selfless act of redemptive love. She has developed a growing prayer life and has found a home in the midst of the community. She is quite sure that God is calling her to become immersed in the baptismal waters of rebirth, to be born anew as his adopted daughter in Christ, to be confirmed in the image and likeness of Jesus Christ and to enter fully into this eucharistic Catholic communion. She is ready to cross the threshold into the next phase of her initiation journey. She is ready to celebrate the Rite of Acceptance.

THE CROSS

Saying yes to Christ ultimately means saying yes to the mystery of suffering and radical discipleship. Christianity immerses us in the pool of paschal love. In the Rite of Acceptance the catechumen promises to "put on" the cross of Christ. Every part of the catechumen's body is signed with the cross of Christ as a reminder that what we see, what we feel, what we hear, where we walk and how we live is overshadowed by the power of the cross of Jesus Christ. We are branded with that cross. We wear it proudly as our badge of honor. We are reminded that the cross of Christ brought life to the world, and our own participation in that cross invites resurrection in our own lives.

THE COMMUNITY

At the Rite of Acceptance, inquirers make the first public ritual gesture asserting their desire to become Christian. They publicly accept the gospel of Christ and are signed with the cross of Christ. Their sponsors and the Christian community, in turn, accept them as members of God's household and promise to support them in their quest and on their journey. The community praises God for inviting the catechumens to enter more fully into his life.

The Rite of Acceptance is an invitation for all of us to renew our commitment to embrace the gospel and to live the paschal mystery in our everyday lives. The optional Rite of Welcome for baptized Christians recognizes the baptismal status of the inquirer. Similar to the Rite of Acceptance, it celebrates passage into the period of the catechumenate.

One important way that the community and the specific initiation ministers offer divine hospitality to those who come seeking is to demonstrate by word and action that we are all on the same journey of conversion. It is a life-long process. Those who minister have not "arrived." The journey is the point. This is not something the minister does to the inquirers, but rather it is a process of conversion that we all share; it is a journey of apprenticeship. When Jesus asks the question, "What do you seek?" Our response is to take the seeker by the hand and say, "Together let us go and see."

CHILDREN AND PRECATECHUMENATE

No separate initiation process prescribed for children who have reached catechetical age (about seven years old) exists. The mistaken impression that there is a separate process for children occurs in part because there are rites in the text especially for children. The crafters of this rite included those rites for the purpose of being sensitive to the developmental needs of children. The rites for children (RCIA, 252–330) are the same rites celebrated with adults, only suited to the age and developmental ability of children. One of the European crafters of the rite was asked why there are separate rituals for children. His response indicated that they were concerned about placing an undue burden on children who are bashful and afraid to get up in front of crowds. He was informed that American children are anything but shy and bashful. He insisted that they should celebrate the same rites the adults celebrate, and when the adults celebrate them.

A primary factor in working with children is the family. Parents must be consulted when their child expresses an interest in full initiation in the church since they must give their explicit consent for the child to go forward for the sacraments (RCIA, 252). An interview at the family home often helps provide a fuller picture of the child and his or her needs.

Involving the family in the initiation process from the very beginning is essential. The parents, the child inquirer and any siblings all participate in the period of the precatechumenate. If the parents are already evangelized, they support the journey of their child. If not, the entire family may enter a process of conversion. Whatever the case, the family should always be made to feel welcome. Social gatherings for the families may foster a sense of welcome. Opportunities for the families to ask questions and journey alongside their child or sibling must always be provided.

When the parents of the child are also seeking Christian initiation, they may participate in the precatechumenate with their child as long as there is ample opportunity for the adult to grow in faith as well. This usually works well, but there are times when the adults need to experience faith in the context of an adult group. Appropriate discernment, creativity and imagination are important to ensure that the needs of both the child and adult are met. In my own particular ministry setting, it is rare that adults and their children are in the precatechumenate at the same time. As a community made up largely of retired people, we have very few children in the process at any given time. On one occasion, however, there did happen to be two families in which both parent and child were in the precatechumenate simultaneously. Rather than participating in the adult precatechumenate sessions, the parents joined their children in the precatechumenate adapted to children. Two catechists worked with the group. When they gathered as a group, the sessions consisted of two major activities—a large group activity and a smaller group activity. In the large group session the children, their parents and the catechists shared their lives in connection with the Christian story. This session was primarily geared to the developmental abilities of the children. In the smaller group sessions, however, the parents formed one group (parents who were themselves inquirers and parents who were already Catholic but were participating with their children in the process) and the children formed another group. A catechist facilitated each group. The children engaged in an evangelization-focused activity suited for them; the parents expanded on the concepts shared in the previous group and discussed them according to their own needs and perspectives.

The initiation of children is built on the same principles as the initiation of adults. Thus, in the period of the precatechumenate, the issues of content, discernment and evangelization are the same.

Some primary issues concerning children in the precatechumenate include

> 1) adapting the evangelization concerns mentioned above for children
>
> 2) sharing stories of faith with the children
>
> 3) providing opportunities for children to share their own stories
>
> 4) sharing stories of faith from the Bible

5) helping children see the work and action of God in their lives

6) helping children develop a loving relationship with Jesus and a positive image of God

7) helping them understand that they are part of a community — not a class.

NOTES

1. "Journey to the Fullness of Life: A Report on the Implementation of the *Rite of Christian Initiation of Adults* in the United States."

2. This certainly mitigates against one Rite of Acceptance a year, celebrated on or near the First Sunday of Advent which results in a catechumenate period lasting only about four months. This hardly embraces the vision of a catechumenate period which encompasses the entire liturgical cycle as envisioned by the rite itself— National Statutes, 6.

CHAPTER 6

The Period of the Catechumenate

The parish celebrates the Rite of Acceptance into the Order of Catechumens with Maureen when she is ready. So begins the pastoral, liturgical formation envisioned in paragraphs 75 to 89 of the RCIA, the "suitable catechesis . . . planned to be gradual and complete in its coverage, accommodated to the liturgical year, and solidly supported by celebrations of the word" (RCIA, 75.1). So begins her liturgical catechesis. So begins the period of the catechumenate.

LITURGICAL CATECHESIS

The term *catechesis* is often misunderstood. Many people believe that catechesis simply means the teaching of religion, primarily by explaining the church's doctrines. Catechesis means much more. Catechesis means to proclaim the person of Jesus Christ and to have that proclamation resound in the hearts and minds of all who will listen and to have them echo back with faith and understanding what they have heard. This proclaiming, resounding and echoing—this catechesis—occurs in the initiation process primarily through liturgical catechesis.

Liturgical catechesis is a term that is often used, but it does not always mean the same thing to everyone. The RCIA is a liturgical rite, thus the context for the catechesis assumed by the rite is liturgical. It flows from the rite, the liturgical year and the celebration of the liturgy. Many people understand liturgical catechesis to be synonymous with lectionary-based catechesis. Lectionary-based catechesis is formation that is centered solely on the Sunday liturgy of the word. As such, it reduces the entire endeavor of catechesis to just one of its parts. Catechesis centered on the lectionary readings is a small, although important, part of liturgical catechesis. Liturgical catechesis is a much broader concept. It is the catechesis envisioned in the *Rite of Christian Initiation of Adults.*

The catechesis assumed in this liturgical rite, which is explicitly outlined in paragraph 75, is four-dimensional: liturgy, word, community and service. No one element is more important than the other is. These four elements together embody the fullness of catechumenal formation. From and within the celebration of the liturgy flows our paschal life, which is rooted in the word of God and the tradition of the church, celebrated and nurtured in the community of the faithful and finds expression in living the apostolic life. Liturgical catechesis assumes that the Christian community apprentices catechumens and candidates in the four elements of initiatory formation—word, liturgy, service and community.

COMMUNAL FORMATION

The community embraces and nurtures catechumens and candidates. Together they worship God in the liturgy; they celebrate God's word and reflect on its meaning. They invoke the Holy Spirit to transform themselves, the catechumens and candidates, the gifts of bread and wine, and the world. The community supports the catechumens and candidates as they celebrate and reflect upon church tradition, which flows from the celebration of the liturgy and the liturgical year. The community walks with them. The community shows them the way to put what they have received into a life of apostolic action and service. The liturgical catechesis of the RCIA empowers the community to do what it was baptized to do: share the Good News of Jesus Christ.

Catechumens are formed in the midst of the worshiping community. They pray with the community and, in turn, learn how to pray. They accompany the community as it feeds the hungry, ministers to the sick and lives the corporal and spiritual works of mercy; in turn they learn to live the Beatitudes. The community observes the Sundays, solemnities and feasts of the liturgical calendar, and, in turn, the candidates for initiation learn to live the life of Christ as it unfolds throughout the year. The community apprentices catechumens in the Christian life.

The community gathers for worship and for community-building events such as parish missions, festivals and outreach to the poor and the world, and in turn catechumens learn what it means to be part of the Body of Christ. They also learn to encounter Jesus in the midst of God's people.

LITURGICAL FORMATION

Liturgical catechesis involves preparation to enter into full, conscious and active participation in the liturgy and mystagogical reflection on the liturgical experience. This reflection leads to an understanding of the sacramental mysteries and to a deeper meaning for one's life. The basis and origin of liturgical catechesis is the liturgical year, the liturgy, the ritual gestures, the symbols of faith, the sacraments and the feasts. Embodied in and flowing from these are the major tenets of our Catholic tradition. The *Constitution on the Sacred Liturgy* reminds us that within the church's liturgical cycle the entire mystery of Christ is unfolded, "from his incarnation and birth until his ascension, the day of Pentecost, and the expectation of blessed hope and of the Lord's return" (CSL, 102).

The documents of the church affirm the power of liturgy to form and transform the people of God. The *Catechism of the Catholic Church* declares that liturgy is the privileged place for catechizing the faithful: "Catechesis is intrinsically linked with the whole of liturgical and sacramental activity, for it is in the sacraments, especially in the eucharist, that Christ Jesus works in fullness for the transformation of [all]" (CCC, 1074). The *Constitution on the Sacred Liturgy* reminds us that liturgy is an important source of catechesis, the "source and summit toward which the activity of the church is directed; at the same time it is the fount from which all the church's power flows"(CSL, 10). It further attests that, "Although the liturgy is above all things the worship of the divine majesty, it likewise contains rich instruction for the faithful" (#33).

The liturgy is pregnant with meaning; it celebrates our Christian story, heritage and faith. Liturgy forms people in the primary truths of our faith. Our Christian identity and our belief systems flow from the church at prayer. Our Catholic way of life—our spiritual and apostolic life—flows from the celebration of the liturgy.

Full and active participation in the liturgy ultimately leads to metanoia. Liturgy's purpose is to transform us more fully into the image of Christ. Liturgical catechesis echoes, resounds and proclaims our relationship with God, with one another and with the world; the primary place where this relationship is celebrated and nurtured is in the liturgy. The church is so insistent on this type of catechesis in the formation of men and women that it is the only way it intends for new members to be initiated. Thus the *Rite of Christian Initiation of Adults* sets forth its intention:

> The instruction that the catechumens receive during this period should be of a kind that while presenting Catholic teaching in its entirety also enlightens faith, directs the heart toward God, fosters participation in the liturgy, inspires apostolic activity, and nurtures a life completely in accord with the Spirit of God. (RCIA, 78)

> During the period of the catechumenate there should be celebrations of the word of God that accord with

the liturgical season and that contribute to the instruction of the catechumens and the needs of the community. These celebrations of the word are: first, celebrations held especially for the catechumens; second, participation in the liturgy of the word at the Sunday Mass; third, celebrations held in connection with catechetical instruction. (#80)

The special celebrations of the word of God arranged for the benefit of the catechumens have as their main purpose

1. to implant in their hearts the teachings they are receiving: for example, the morality characteristic of the New Testament, the forgiving of injuries and insults, a sense of sin and repentance, the duties Christians must carry out in the world;

2. to give them instruction and experience in the different aspects and ways of prayer;

3. to explain to them the signs, celebrations, and seasons of the liturgy;

4. to prepare them to gradually enter the worship assembly of the entire community. (#82)

It is very clear that the formation catechumens are to receive flows from the liturgy. Liturgical catechesis is less concerned with knowledge and information, though it includes it; it is more concerned with conversion, transformation and formation.

Liturgical catechesis draws its life and flows primarily from the liturgical year and the Sunday eucharist celebrated within its context. The entire Christ event, the basis of catechumenal formation, is celebrated in one complete liturgical cycle. The fullness of the Christian story is not only celebrated in the Sunday experience. It is also reflected in the celebration of the sacraments, solemnities, holy days and the octaves of Christmas and Easter.

The celebration of the liturgy of the word in one complete liturgical cycle is the primary formation of catechumens (National Statutes, 6). They are formed in the life and mission of Christ. The principal place where that life and mission is remembered and made present is in the liturgy, within the context of the liturgical seasons. The entire mystery of Christ is celebrated in the liturgical year from the announcement of his birth, his incarnation, his life, passion, death and resurrection and the sending of the Holy Spirit. From the celebration of Christ's life in the context of the liturgy flows the fullness of Catholic Christian belief. Thus, the catechumenate proper is to last at least one full year from the time the catechumen celebrates the Rite of Acceptance.

Thus, week after week our catechumen Maureen celebrates the liturgy of the word with the entire community and is "kindly dismissed" after the homily to reflect further on the entire liturgy of the word—symbols, ritual prayers, readings, music and homily—within the context of the liturgical season.

CATECHETICAL FORMATION

The liturgy catechizes in a myriad of ways. One primary way it catechizes is through the scripture readings appointed for each Sunday, feast and sacramental celebration. When the word is proclaimed in the celebrating assembly, it is as if Jesus Christ himself were proclaiming that word. Christ is truly present to teach, encourage, console, affirm and challenge the people of God. We actively listen to God's word and to the homily that breaks that word open in order to find meaning for our everyday lives. Catechumens are dismissed to reflect further on that word. Their reflection is brought into dialogue with sound biblical scholarship. Because we lack the background to understand what the biblical texts meant to first-century listeners, we draw upon the biblical interpretation (exegesis) provided by faithful, contemporary scholarship. Exegesis expands our understanding of the text and helps us appropriate the meaning so that we can live the gospel more fully in our everyday lives.

Another way the liturgy catechizes is through its ritual texts. The entrance antiphons, opening prayers, prefaces, eucharistic prayers and communion prayers are filled with powerful images, biblical references and metaphors. They deserve our thoughtful, prayerful attention and reflection. The liturgical texts also shed light on the liturgical season, the Sundays, feasts and sacramental celebrations. They proclaim and articulate our Catholic theology. One needs look no further than the prefaces for Christmas to find the most beautiful articulation of our theology of the Incarnation.

Through the symbols particular to each celebration, the liturgy catechizes the primary symbols of our faith and the ritual gestures and symbolic actions that accompany those symbols. Symbols express our Catholic Christian identity; they tell our story in ways that words cannot. The light of the Easter candle says we are children of the Light who continue to follow that Light on our life's journey. The gathered community proclaims that we are the Body of Christ, the People of God, and that Christ is present in our midst. The cross in our church announces that we are people of the cross who are willing to offer our joys, sorrows and struggles for the sake of others and who embrace the paschal mystery in our everyday lives. The beautiful gospel book carried reverently in procession affirms that we are people of the word who listen, reflect and act on God's word. The baptismal symbols of flowing water and the white garment declare us to be people immersed in life-giving water who have put on Christ. We cooperate with God's work of re-creation in our lives, and through our baptismal promises we recommit ourselves to living more fully as priest, prophet and king. We are people who continue to call upon God's Spirit through the laying on of hands and who have been anointed and sealed with the oil of the Spirit. Finally, we are people who take, bless, break and share the bread of life and the cup of salvation. We receive Christ in the eucharist under these signs; we become what we have received so we can go out and share it with the world.

Paragraph 75.1 directs that there is to be a suitable, complete and gradual catechesis, "accommodated to the liturgical year and solidly supported by celebrations of the word." It is to lead catechumens to "an appropriate acquaintance with dogma and precepts." Paragraphs 81 to 84 reaffirm and clarify this catechetical formation further. Some of the celebrations of the word should take place on Sunday in keeping with the command to keep the Lord's Day holy. The catechumens participate in the liturgy of the word and then are "kindly dismissed." They may also participate in catechetical or instructional meetings within the context of celebrations of the word in order that such instruction is rooted in prayer.

What are the practical implications of these directives? There is no absolute formula. The rite gives a great deal of latitude to adapt catechumenal formation to suit the pastoral and cultural needs of any given ministry setting. The rite does, however, present us with the key elements of catechetical formation:

— Celebrations of the word

— Attention to the liturgical year

— Participation in the Sunday liturgy of the word

— Dismissal from the liturgy of the word

— Catechetical or instructional meetings

It is clear that the locus of catechumenal formation is the liturgy—celebrations of the word, liturgies of the word, the liturgical year and dismissal from the liturgy. Since the word celebrated at the Sunday liturgy is the primary catechumenal formation, reflection on that liturgy (in the context of the liturgical year) and the scriptures are a critical component. From that experience of liturgy flows the Christian, Catholic way of life—what we believe and how we are to live. Catechumens are "kindly dismissed" to examine and reflect on their experience of liturgy and the word. In doing so, catechumens are formed in what will, it is hoped, become a habit for the rest of their lives: celebration which leads to reflection, which leads to meaning for one's life, which leads to a decision to live in a new and transformed way. Through this process of reflection a person allows the liturgy to transform his or her life; through it both catechumens and faithful learn what it is we believe and how we are to live what we have learned.

DISMISSAL CATECHESIS

How does this work in a parish setting? Catechumens celebrate the Sunday liturgy of the word with the community. They are dismissed after the homily to break open the word, as the rite directs (RCIA, 67).

Some people object to the dismissal. They fear it communicates that the catechumens are being ignored, not taken seriously or treated inhospitably. To some, the dismissal communicates that the catechumen is unworthy to stay for the liturgy of the eucharist.

What are the reasons for the dismissal? First, there is a clear distinction between the ecclesial status of catechumen and of the faithful. The faithful are fed at the table of God's word and the table of the eucharist. Catechumens are fed at the table of God's word in preparation for the day when, through baptism, they will take their place at the table of the eucharist. Thus, the primary formation for catechumens is the word and reflection on that word.

Second, when we are at the table of the eucharist we are feasting at the Lord's Supper. Would anyone invite someone to their house for dinner, gather around the family table, share family stories, and then say, "You will not be eating with us tonight, but please sit there with us while we eat our dinner"? The answer is obvious. In that same spirit, why would we invite a catechumen to this holy meal in which he or she is not able to participate? It is a question of hospitality.

Third, the tradition of dismissal from the liturgy of the word is so important that the word that we use to this day, *Mass*, is derived from the Latin root for the word *dismissal.* The origins of the word suggest being sent *to* something, rather than *from* something. Dismissal at Sunday eucharist is a dismissal to go out into the world to become eucharist for others and to share the Good News. Dismissal from the word is a dismissal to go out to reflect upon and to become God's word in one's life.

After their dismissal, where the catechumens go varies from setting to setting. Some parishes send the catechumens with a catechist to another space on the parish grounds, and for the duration of the liturgy they break open the word just celebrated. When further catechetical or doctrinal instruction is desired, there is varied practice as well. Some parishes will extend the catechesis as sponsors join the catechumens after Mass. Catechumens and sponsors will then spend another hour or so exploring church tradition and teaching. In other places catechumens leave for home after they have broken open the word and then return on another day for further catechesis. When they return, the word is proclaimed again (see RCIA, 85–89, for a model), followed by further catechetical instruction, thus making the connection between liturgy and the tradition of the church.

Nowhere in the rite does it say that further catechetical instruction should take place every week. Additional catechetical instruction beyond celebration and reflection on the word is a dimension of catechumenal formation—a big dimension—but it shares times and space with the other dimensions named in paragraph 75. Sometimes candidates for initiation will participate in the apostolic, liturgical and communal dimensions of their intended formation.

Some parishes are unable to dismiss catechumens to another place because they lack the luxury of additional meeting space. In this case, they may be dismissed for the day to return on another day, or they may stay for the rest of the liturgy, with an exhortation that this is an anticipation of the future, when they will participate fully in the eucharist (RCIA, 67, option C).

When the catechumens return on another day, they celebrate the word that was proclaimed on Sunday (see RCIA, 85–89), and they break open that word. If further catechetical instruction is to follow, catechumens will remain to share our Catholic tradition. Various ministry settings should make whatever adaptations are needed to provide appropriate catechumenal formation.

Methodologies for breaking open the word may also vary. However, common elements important to the process are celebration of the word, the catechumen's personal experience of the word, biblical interpretation of the word, and dialogue and decision for action.

EXTENDED CATECHESIS

There are times when further catechetical instruction takes place for the purpose of passing on Catholic dogma and precepts. This doctrinal formation is an essential and integral part of the formation of catechumens, but it is not the primary focus. There is a reason the church placed Christian initiation within the context of a liturgical rite. It speaks volumes about how the church understands the formation that is needed to prepare people for a lifetime of discipleship.

If the church were concerned with nothing but imparting Catholic doctrine, the chief means of initiating would be to hand out the catechism. Instead, the church has a liturgical rite and desires that the catechesis emanating from it be liturgical, initiatory and evangelical in context and nature. (Please refer to Appendix I, "Doctrine and the Catechumenate," at the end of this book. It elaborates more fully on the place of doctrine within the catechumenal process.)

APOSTOLIC FORMATION

Unfortunately, the apostolic element of catechumenal formation is often talked about but otherwise ignored. But the apostolic formation of catechumens is where the proverbial rubber meets the road. The life of apostolic service is the way that the challenges prompted by communal, liturgical, scriptural and doctrinal formation are put into practice. The apostolic life is not simply a matter for discussion; it is to be lived. This is where communal formation and apostolic formation meet. The community assumes its baptismal role and invites the catechumen to walk with it into the world to live the Beatitudes and to spread the Good News.

Thus, apostolic formation assumes that the catechumen is out in the trenches with other members of the Christian community, feeding the hungry, sheltering the homeless and tending to the sick and the lonely. She is an apprentice in the Christian life. She does not simply hear about the Christian life; her formation demands that she live it, walk it and make its practice part of the fabric of her life.

BAPTIZED CANDIDATES

The formation laid out in the preceding sections is normative for unbaptized, uncatechized persons. It should extend for one complete liturgical cycle from the time the catechumens celebrate the Rite of Acceptance until their initiation at the Easter Vigil at least one year later.

What then about baptized candidates? Baptized candidates, raised in another ecclesial tradition and fully active in that tradition, who wish to become Catholic are not bound by the principles in this rite. They may need a brief period of sacramental preparation and catechetical instruction concerning the differences between the two traditions before they celebrate a Rite of Reception into the Full Communion of the Catholic Church, but the rite insists that no unnecessary burden be placed on them.

What about baptized candidates with no religious or spiritual background or history? While they are in union with us through their baptism, there is little difference between such a candidate and a catechumen:

> Even though these uncatechized adults have not yet
> heard the message of the mystery of Christ, their sta-
> tus differs from that of catechumens, since by bap-
> tism they have already become members of the
> church and children of God. Hence their conversion
> is based on the baptism they have already received,
> the effects of which they must develop. (RCIA, 400)

The rite recognizes that these candidates need a considerable time of
preparation. The rite further suggests that this preparation is parallel
to the preparation provided for catechumens and points ministers to
paragraph 75 and following for direction concerning the formation
they should receive.

Some parishes provide separate formation programs for baptized and unbaptized candidates. Many parishes, however, have effectively incorporated both the baptized and unbaptized into one
process, while being careful to respect and honor the baptism of those
who are already baptized.

Baptized candidates possess varying degrees of prior formation.
Many are somewhat catechized, but need a degree of preparation and
probation. The length of formation for somewhat catechized, baptized persons depends on the extent to which those persons are catechized. To discern when someone is fully catechized, the ministers
ask, What does it mean to be catechized? While there is no formal
answer to this question, we get a glimpse of the fullness of catechesis
when we explore what church documents have to tell us about the
nature of catechesis.

Discerning What It Means to Be Catechized

The catechetical documents of the church set forth what the fullness
of catechesis entails. All of the documents combined suggest a fullness of catechesis that few people possess. These documents do, however, serve as a guide, an ideal to strive for and a direction to lead all
whose responsibility it is to catechize the people of God.

The *National Catechetical Directory*, (NCD), the *General Directory for Catechesis*, (GDC) and the *Rite of Christian Initiation of Adults* (RCIA) point to what full and complete catechesis means. The NCD reminds us that people are catechized through natural signs. God is revealed through creation, one another, in everyday life, in art, science, music and technology. Thus, catechized persons are people who are aware of the presence and revelation of God in our temporal world. The NCD further affirms that we are catechized through biblical, ecclesial and liturgical signs as well. Thus, catechized persons read and pray the scriptures. They have a sense of the living word of God and understand the scriptures as the inspired word of God. They understand that scripture comprises various literary genres and so they do not accept a fundamentalist view of the Bible.

Catechized people have a sense of the life, creed and practice of the church throughout the ages up to the present generation. The NCD further asserts that catechized people possess an appreciation for the role of liturgy; that it is the source and summit of all we do as Christians (NCD, 36, 44).

The *General Directory for Catechesis* (GDC, 85–86) indicates that the primary task of catechesis is to promote knowledge of the faith, liturgical education and moral formation. Catechesis accomplishes that task by teaching people to pray, forming them in the life of the community, and encouraging a missionary spirit. Thus, catechized persons are imbued with a basic knowledge of the faith. They have an appreciation of liturgy and strive to participate fully and actively. They commit themselves to the continuing journey of conversion. They strive to live the Beatitudes, and they understand the social consequences of gospel imperatives. Catechized people understand the importance of community and embrace their responsibility to share the Good News. They are committed to a life of prayer, both liturgical and personal.

The RCIA (75) sets forth the dimensions of catechesis, thus providing us with indicators that describe the nature of catechesis and what to look for when discerning who is catechized, and who might need further catechesis. The same principles mentioned above are named: formation in word, in liturgy, the service and apostolic life and community.

Those who are catechized have a sense that scripture brings to bear not only each person's original experience and hearing of the word, but also the church's understanding of that word. They embrace the truths embodied in the Nicene Creed, the Lord's Prayer, the sacramental life of the church, the Beatitudes and the Ten Commandments, which are celebrated in liturgy. They understand that they are baptized into ministry and service. Catechized persons live their baptismal role of priest, prophet and king. Thus, they serve God's people, they take the word of God out into the world and they lead people to Christ. Catechized persons understand that the mission of Christianity is apostolic by nature and that the gospel commits us to the work of peace, charity and justice, especially toward the poor and marginalized.

Catechized individuals understand that Christianity is lived in community, that the community is a sign and symbol of the presence of Christ in the world, and that it is both human and divine. Catechized persons also understand that liturgy is the source and summit of all Christian activity and the font from which our power flows, and that Christian life is celebrated, professed and embodied in worship, sacraments, liturgical signs, and the liturgical year. Catechized people have the sense that liturgy calls us to mission in the world.

THE CANDIDATES

Few people who knock on our catechumenal doors possess the fullness of catechesis just described. There are some, however, who possess various degrees of catechesis. Their formation is determined by the level of catechesis they already possess and by the areas where catechesis is lacking. One of the roles of an effective catechumenal minister is to discern the degree to which a person is catechized when seeking initiation or full communion. These criteria are indicators that will gradually become apparent as the person journeys through the process.

Once it is determined that candidates belong in the period of the catechumenate, the length of their formation depends on the extent of their catechesis. Many baptized persons who enter the processes of initiation are minimally catechized. They may know and love Jesus, but beyond that there is little religious training to build upon. The path for such folks is parallel to that of the catechumen: one complete liturgical cycle.

What about those who come to us who possess varying degrees of catechesis? When appropriate adult learning models are used, it soon becomes apparent where the missing pieces lie in a person's catechetical formation.

A few composite examples will help illustrate the various levels of catechesis among the baptized candidates. The names and some situations have been changed to protect the anonymity of the candidates. Sam was a baptized, active Lutheran; he was a deacon and youth minister in his church. It appeared at first glance that Sam was completely catechized. He was fully aware of the ecclesial differences between the Lutheran and Catholic churches. Half of his family was Catholic, so he was very much at home in the Catholic church. Sam did not belong in the catechumenate. He just needed a brief period of sacramental preparation that we did not provide at the time Sam was in the process.[1] After a few weeks in the process it was evident that Sam should be received into the Catholic church. He was catechized in every sense of the word—or so we thought. Sam, however, insisted that there was a piece missing for him. He was struggling with Catholic social teaching. He wanted more time to grow in acceptance of this very important church teaching. After a few months Sam told us that he had worked through the obstacle and was ready to be received. We celebrated the Rite of Reception with him at a Sunday liturgy.

Pete was a Baptist. His mother was a Catholic so Pete was very much at home in the Catholic church. When Pete came to us, he had been attending the Catholic church for about six months and was already involved in the life of the community. He formed a men's prayer group at his place of work and he was enthusiastic in his zeal to share the Good News with others. He had a suitable acquaintance with Catholic dogmas and precepts. Pete's fundamentalist background was so deeply rooted in him, however, that he simply could not move beyond a strict fundamental and literalist hearing and understanding of scripture. Pete remained in the process for about six months—longer than anyone anticipated. He needed continuous immersion in God's word in the context of worship, reflection and sound biblical scholarship. His resistance finally melted and Pete was received at a Sunday liturgy when it was discerned by him and by the catechumenal community that he was ready to complete his sacramental initiation.

Jean attended church weekly in the Episcopal church. She had very little connection with her community. However, Jean read the Bible every day. She had more than an adequate acquaintance with Catholic dogma and precepts and was aware of the unique differences between her previous tradition and Catholicism. Sunday worship was an integral part of her life. Jean never participated in her community's social or outreach activities. Her relationship to church was a private, personal affair. It was discerned that Jean needed a period of time to share life, scripture and tradition with the community. Jean did spend a brief period of time in the catechumenal process. Her sponsor made sure that Jean participated in all the parish social activities, inviting Jean to accompany her when she visited the sick and ministered to the poor through her involvement in the St. Vincent de Paul Society. Jean became involved in a small faith-sharing group and was part of a group that made bagged lunches for the homeless. Then after a few months in the process, Jean was received into full communion at a Sunday liturgy.

George was baptized as an infant but never had further exposure to a church community. George was in the catechumenate for about a year and was received into full communion during the Easter season.

Tim was a baptized person who attended weekly Mass with his family for over twenty years. He was very involved in the parish. Tim and his wife prepared engaged couples for marriage. They were involved in a small Christian community. He participated in sacramental preparation programs for all of his children throughout the years. Tim was the president of the parish school board and was a profoundly religious man, deeply immersed in the life of the community. He participated in every parish mission, retreat and enrichment program offered by the parish. He was invited to be on the parish stewardship committee and to be a facilitator for a major renewal program in the parish. Tim was also active in many of the parish outreach programs. Tim finally resolved his self-imposed obstacle to becoming a Catholic and decided that the time had finally arrived. Tim did not need catechumenal formation. We prepared him for the celebration of confirmation and eucharist, and two weeks after he told us that he was ready, he entered into the full communion of the Catholic church at a Sunday liturgy.

Sally, Rachel and John were Catholics who never celebrated the sacrament of confirmation when they were young. They were active members of the community and simply wanted to complete their sacraments. They met with the couple that prepares catechized people for the sacraments of confirmation and eucharist. The three Catholics were prepared a few weeks before the bishop was scheduled to come to the parish for the celebration of confirmation.

Kathy was baptized Catholic as an infant but was never raised Catholic. She received no religious formation whatsoever. Kathy's formation was parallel to that of the catechumen (National Statutes, 25). The RCIA affirms that Kathy's "conversion is based on the baptism [she] already received, the effects of which [she] must develop" (RCIA, 400). Paragraph 401 refers to the formation set forth for catechumens in paragraphs 75 and following. The formation for uncatechized baptized persons "corresponds to the one laid down for catechumens." The RCIA also insists that such candidates would benefit from the celebration of liturgical rites belonging to the period of the catechumenate. Thus, Kathy completed her sacraments of confirmation and eucharist during the Easter season, approximately one year after she entered the period of the catechumenate. Kathy participated in an evening of baptismal remembrance celebrated with all the baptized candidates in which the baptism of the candidates was remembered and honored. Great care was shown throughout Kathy's journey to acknowledge her status as a baptized Catholic.

Patricia was a baptized Methodist—or so we thought. She was not going to need a full year of formation, but considerable time was needed. Her participation in the Methodist church was not consistent throughout the years, and there were many missing pieces in her religious formation. After about seven months in the process, it was discerned that Patricia was ready to come into the full communion of the Catholic church. Shortly before the scheduled date for the rite of reception, though, she learned the truth about her baptism. After months of trying to get her baptismal certificate from her mother, her mother was embarrassed to admit that they never had Patricia baptized. Throughout her life, Patricia thought she was baptized. She was ready and eager to become a Catholic. There was no sense in making her wait until the Easter Vigil. Patricia was baptized under the Exceptional Circumstances (RCIA, 331–339) provision in the rite, and at a Sunday liturgy in October, Patricia was fully immersed in the life-giving waters of baptism. She was confirmed and received her first communion.

Billy was a 14-year-old unbaptized, uncatechized young man who was too mature to be in our process for children. Billy suffered more in the two years he was in the process than most people do in their entire lives. His father, who had custody of Billy, died suddenly. Billy was left in the care of his stepmother, who loves him very much but who had no legal right to care for him. His drug-addicted birth mother, who has had no relationship with the boy, thought there was government money to be gleaned. She kidnapped him, took him out of state and forced him to live in deplorable conditions. He ran away from the situation, and was placed in a mental institution by the authorities until things could be worked out. His stepmother was awarded temporary guardianship, and Billy was returned to her. He subsequently returned to the initiation process.

The stories of cross and resurrection that he shares with the catechumenal group does more for the formation of the adults than it does for Billy. We have all been deeply touched by stories Billy has shared about the sustaining power of God to see him through his darkest days. If Billy had followed the normal course of this process, he would probably have been initiated at the Easter Vigil a year ago. He has been in and out of the process for prolonged periods because of the circumstances of his life. Billy will be baptized, confirmed and receive communion at the Easter Vigil this year. The beauty of a catechumenate that never ends is that people whose life circumstances take them out of the process are able to continue where they left off without missing a beat.

CHILDREN AND THE CATECHUMENATE

The *Rite of Christian Initiation of Adults* includes children of catechetical age; part II, section I, of the rite treats the initiation of children as one particular circumstance of initiation. There is no separate process. Although some parishes refer to the "RCIC" (rite of Christian initiation of children) and even "RCIT" (for teens), they do not exist. Preparation for sacramental initiation for children is based on the same principles as the preparation of adults and on the same document. The only difference is that the formation for children is suited to their age and developmental needs.

The period of the catechumenate is much the same for children as it is for adults. Children are dismissed from the liturgy at the same time as the adults.[2] They too break open the word, and if there is to be a further instructional gathering, the parents join the children after Mass. When the parents of the children are also in the catechumenate, the parents either participate with the children in breaking open the word and then join the adults after Mass for extended catechesis or stay with the adults for both breaking open the word and extended catechesis. Adapting to the needs of each community requires much creativity and imagination.

Sixty-five percent of the people in our parish are retired. Therefore, we rarely have more than ten children a year in the overall process. When we have young teens that do not belong in our children's process, we include them in our adult process. A second catechist is appointed just for them. When the adult group shares, the teens form their own group, and under the facilitation of a catechist, they make their own appropriate connections. The key to working with children and teens, or any particular group, is to adapt to the circumstances at hand. What one parish does to accommodate ten children a year will hardly be sufficient for a parish that ministers to fifty in the same year.

As stated earlier, the same principles for the catechumenate apply to ministry with children. When the catechists in my parish meet for the monthly meeting of catechumenate catechists, the catechists who work with the children also participate. What we do with adults, we do with children, scaled to their age and developmental ability.

For children, as well as adults, the catechumenate is a time to enter more deeply into the life of conversion and transformation in the midst of the celebrating community. It is a time to be formed in the Christian life. The RCIA states that this formation flows from the Sunday liturgy, and the stories of Jesus that are told in the course of the liturgical year. The RCIA insists that the formation just described is the best way to form Catholic Christians.

The catechumenate is a time for immersion in the symbols that give us our identity—light, cross, community, fire, water, garment, oil, bread and wine. Children and adults apprentice the Christian life by their participation in the life of the community—by prayer and by living the gospel and by doing the work Jesus commanded us to do.

Children become acquainted with the precepts found in the Apostles' Creed. They are introduced to the same principles that the adults encounter throughout the celebration of the liturgical year. The catechumenate begins the ongoing formation in the Christian life that will continue throughout the life of the child. The goal of the catechumenate for both children and adults is radical conversion and transformation.

DISMISSAL CATECHESIS FOR BAPTIZED CANDIDATES?

The question of whether or not to dismiss baptized candidates arouses strong opinions on both sides of the issue. It appears that the rite does not intend for baptized candidates to be dismissed with the catechumens after the liturgy of the word. They should remain for the rest of the Mass. When looking at the rites for baptized candidates, there is no dismissal provided. While there is presently serious study and dialogue going on over this issue, I would like to address it from my own pastoral experience.

While uncatechized, baptized candidates do enjoy a special status as baptized individuals ("their conversion is based on the baptism they have already received, the effects of which they must develop" [RCIA, 400]), their formation needs are virtually no different from that of the baptized. Most parishes do not have the resources to provide two separate formation processes for uncatechized, baptized and unbaptized individuals. While the rite makes no provision for the dismissal of baptized candidates, a credible argument can be made for doing so. Paragraphs 400 to 410 insist on maintaining the unique needs of the baptized candidates, but when it comes to their formation, the rite refers back to paragraphs 75 to 89 for the model their formation is to follow. In that model, the primary means of formation is rooted in dismissal catechesis. National Statutes, 31 insists that the candidates may participate in celebrations of the word with catechumens. One might argue that those are separate and distinct from the Sunday experience, and perhaps that is the intention. However, if that statute points to the importance of participating with catechumens in celebrations of the word, the primary place where that takes place is the Sunday liturgy of the word, dismissal and breaking open the word that follows.

John Huels, in his book *The Catechumenate and the Law*, states the reason why baptized candidates are not dismissed. He asserts that when we do not dismiss baptized candidates, when they remain for the liturgy of the eucharist, we are making a powerful statement that baptism does indeed make a difference:

> In the early church, catechumens were dismissed after the liturgy of the word because the sacraments, the sacred "mysteries," were a carefully guarded secret open only to the initiated. Unlike catechumens, candidates for reception into full communion are already baptized and thus are capable of participating, to the extent allowed by law, in the sacraments of the church. Although they may not yet, as a rule, receive holy communion, the candidates' presence is a clear way of signifying that they are already members of the faithful, though they are not yet in full communion. Their presence at the liturgy of the eucharist would be a strong affirmation of the dignity of their baptism in their original church, and a clear sign to them, to the catechumens, and to the entire community that baptism does indeed make a difference.[3]

Huels also says, however, that while the sign value is a good reason for the candidate to remain, they are not bound by law to remain (canon 1247). He reminds us that some places are unable to provide two separate formation processes for both baptized and unbaptized candidates. Thus, he asserts that if baptized candidates are to be dismissed, they be dismissed separately so their baptismal status is noted and affirmed. Another point worthy of consideration is that the rite does not specifically state that the baptized may not be dismissed. Liturgical law assumes that what is not specifically stated is optional.

Pastoral experience tells me that while the sign value is indeed a worthy issue, it does not outweigh the benefits the candidates receive from the experience of breaking open the word on Sunday with the catechumens. The formation received when the catechumens are dismissed to break open the word does more to foster conversion than any other catechumenal activity. When the word is explored deeply in this manner, the gospel comes to life and is connected to the lived experience of those preparing for initiation. Candidates are given the opportunity to allow the word to penetrate deeply and thus to be converted, which, in turn, leads to transformed behavior and action.

Baptized candidates might not be dismissed in situations where the parish dismisses catechumens to their homes to return on another day to break open Sunday's word. In that case, the baptized candidates perhaps would not be dismissed, but would return on the alternate day and join the catechumens (unless there is a separate process for baptized candidates) as they break open the word.

The baptized candidates in my parish are informed that they have a right to stay for the liturgy of the eucharist, but they are nonetheless invited to participate in dismissal catechesis if they so choose. In eight years, only one candidate chose to remain and for purely personal reasons, none of which was sign value.

MANAGING THE PROCESS

If baptized candidates celebrate a rite of reception when it is discerned they are ready to celebrate it, then those rites are celebrated in the parish throughout the year.[4] When an unbaptized, fully catechized person is ready to be initiated, he or she is baptized under the "exceptional circumstances" provision in rite (part II, section 2; see RCIA, 331, 336–339) following all the norms set forth in those paragraphs: at a Sunday liturgy.

Uncatechized, unbaptized individuals spend at least one complete liturgical cycle in the process and are initiated at the Easter Vigil. That means that sometimes those same individuals will be in the process longer than one year. For example, let us return to our catechumen Maureen. Suppose Maureen arrived on our doorstep in October. Suppose further that Maureen had absolutely no religious training in her background. Maureen might have been in the precatechumenate for eight to ten weeks. That means Maureen would be ready to celebrate the Rite of Acceptance sometime in December or early January. She would obviously not be ready for initiation at the Easter Vigil; she would not have been in the process for at least one complete, liturgical cycle. She would therefore remain a catechumen through Easter and wait until at least the following Easter Vigil to be initiated. Our "fast-food" culture sometimes balks at the thought of being in the process for that length of time, but it has been my experience that the candidates themselves (to a person) thanked us for the length of time. One neophyte commented that he is not sure that the Catholic way of life would have taken root as deeply in him had he not been in the process for 16 months. Studies show that conversion to anything requires at least one year of formation in the thing being converted to.

We have had the situation where a candidate was not going to be ready for the Easter Vigil, but perhaps would be ready by Pentecost. In those rare instances, the catechumen participated in the period of purification and enlightenment and then was baptized at a Sunday liturgy on the feast of Pentecost.

If people move through the process according to their own timetables, then how does a parish manage and discern readiness? Discernment is an ongoing process.[5] When candidates break open the word, live the life of service, are immersed in the life of the community and participate in catechetical instruction and reflection, it becomes apparent how and if they were touched by those experiences.

For example, we invited our catechumens and candidates to participate in an evangelization outreach we were doing in our local community. We formed teams and went door to door to invite folks to come and be part of our church family if they did not have one and to offer a neighborly gesture of good will. It was fascinating. We gathered afterward to reflect on the experience. One candidate was so touched that she felt called to the work of evangelization. Another woman hated the experience and found it to be extremely difficult. When asked to articulate a theology of evangelization from their experience, they named most of the principles found in the church's documents on evangelization, much to my amazement. Their theology was not gleaned from a formal teaching on the subject, but from their lived experience.

The woman who hated the experience had been rejected and treated rather rudely at one of the homes. This led to a discussion about the paschal mystery and about the difficulties and the cost of evangelization. Another woman could see the value to a well-lived life in the work of evangelization; she wisely asked, "Could we not do more by just living as good Christians?" That launched a discussion about *Evangelii Nuntiandi* and other church documents on evangelization that teach that evangelization is both living the life and going out to tell others about the life. Every person who participated in the experience was deeply moved by it. Everyone had a greater appreciation of the baptismal call to go out and share the Good News.

That experience was imbued with all the elements of catechumenal formation. The scriptures that day centered on the disciples who were sent out two by two. The community sent us forth with its blessing (formation in liturgy and the word). This was an event in which the catechumens and candidates participated with the community (communal formation) in this evangelization effort (apostolic formation).

We gathered afterward to process the experience and to formulate our understanding about the experience. We discussed the church's teaching on the subject and how our attitudes and decisions were or were not influenced by the experience. It was catechumenal formation at its finest.

When people discuss their decision for changed behaviors and attitudes as part of the normal sequence of events, week after week, catechists and sponsors are readily able to discern what formation is still needed in the life of the candidate. Imagine for a moment, that an individual who participated in that experience were to say, "Personally, I do not believe that I have a responsibility to share my faith with anyone. I see it as personal, between God and me. It is no one else's business." When appropriate, adult-oriented formation practice is going on, the area where growth is needed becomes acutely obvious.

The story of Pete, the Baptist candidate whose fundamentalist way of reading scripture suggested that he needed a longer period of Catholic formation, demonstrates how discernment is an ongoing dynamic. It was quite obvious from Pete's experience with scripture that he was not ready to come into full communion. He simply could not embrace Catholic biblical teaching. Pete's background could have pointed us to the possibility that he would have a problem in that area, but it was not until we shared the scriptures in dialogue with exegesis that it became apparent that movement would be slow for him.

MINISTRIES

During the period of the catechumenate, the entire array of ministries is active. Each of them plays an important role in the formation of catechumens and candidates in the Catholic way of life.

CATECHISTS

Like all the ministers of initiation, the catechist is first and foremost an active, believing member of the Christian community and understands that the community is the one who forms and initiates. He or she knows the parish and its parishioners and is able to tap their wisdom by inviting them to come and share their stories of discipleship with the candidates and by asking those same parishioners to invite candidates to accompany them as they live the gospel in the world and marketplace.

The catechist understands that the life of the community—and so formation into the life of the community—is grounded in its liturgy. She or he has prayed the scriptures and liturgical texts, preferably in communion with other members of the community and/or catechists, prior to gathering with the candidates. If further catechetical instruction emanates from the liturgy, the catechist presents the tradition of the church by connecting it to the lived experience of the candidates. The catechist is skilled in asking the questions that challenge attitudes and ways of looking at and behaving in the world. The catechist knows how to ask the "so what" questions, not just about the scriptures and applying them to daily life, but the church's tradition as well.

The catechist knows that the Christian life is apostolic; it is faith in action. Thus the catechist teaches "about" social justice only after "doing" social justice and also "listening" to others who have been doing it for a long time, then reflecting on the experience afterward by asking

1) What did you experience?

2) What did it teach you about God, church, community, self?

3) As a result of your experience, what would you say the church teaches about the subject?

4) How are you changed as a result of your experience, and what do you want to concretely do about it?

In a catechumenate that is ongoing, never-ending, continuous week after week, year after year, how does a catechist keep from burning out? One catechist can't. Forming potential members must be shared ministry. In our two-thousand-family parish we have the luxury of forming a number of catechists to serve in the period of the catechumenate. We have six regular catechists and other people who participate less regularly. For example, one woman does not want to be regularly committed to a schedule; she retired a few years ago and joined our parish when she moved to Florida. She has been a director of religious education, working with parents to prepare families for the sacraments. She has a beautiful approach to the sacraments and is willing to share that with the candidates for initiation on an occasional basis.

Some catechists develop an expertise in specific areas that interest them. They always ask to be the catechist who will address those specific areas. Their expertise enriches the catechumens' experience.

The catechists are very flexible. There is no set schedule. We gather as a group for a monthly meeting. At that meeting we pray the scriptures, discuss the candidates and then determine what we will do each week for the month ahead. The liturgies for the coming month point us to issues of Catholic faith and life. When we determine what those issues are, we decide if there will be an additional instructional meeting (extended catechesis), or if we will participate in a community activity such as a parish mission, or an apostolic activity such as serving in the local soup kitchen. We would then reflect on the experience afterward by placing it in the context of the church's social teaching.

If there are baptized candidates who might be coming into full communion in the near future, we ask ourselves where formation is still needed in the lives of those persons. We also ask what is going on in the lives of the candidates themselves to determine what we need to do with them for the coming month.

In an ideal world catechists would be able to walk into the weekly session prepared to address any issue that might have emanated from the liturgy that day or week. However, our parish is not the ideal world. The catechists need preparation time for themselves and some sense of where they will be leading their candidates. Thus, we determine what we will do for one month at a time with the understanding that we will change direction if circumstances dictate that we should.

For example, one month the catechists gathered to determine what they would do with the candidates for the coming month. For one of the approaching weeks the liturgy was full of images that begged that we address the issue of social justice. Some activity was planned centered around this theme. During the week we received a call that the infant son of one of our candidates was dying from a rare, but always fatal, disease. Instead of doing something centered around social justice, the circumstances led us into a discussion about the paschal mystery—the mystery of life and death—and our call to participate in Christ's death and suffering. We are to lift up those who suffer. On Sunday, when the liturgy was alive with images of social justice, the catechumenate group reached out to a man and his family. They participated in his suffering by offering to bring meals to his house every day throughout his ordeal. They mowed his lawn, cleaned his house or did whatever they could to ensure that he could spend every precious moment with his son, not doing the menial tasks of life.

This effort spread out to the entire parish. For one year that family did not cook a meal or mow a lawn. When their son died, the catechumenal community shared hours of prayer through the night as his body was brought to the church to lie in vigil prior to the celebration of his funeral.

Here is a second example. At another monthly meeting it was discussed how one of the candidates was persecuted at home for his decision to become a Catholic. The burden was tremendous. The catechists decided that we needed at some point to address the cost of discipleship. We looked to the liturgies of the month ahead to see if any of them addressed the issue of discipleship more pointedly than the others. Once the liturgy was chosen, we decided to invite a wonderful man from the parish who had known great suffering in communist Cuba. He was jailed for two years for insisting on getting married in the Catholic church. He and his family nearly starved and drowned, escaping to religious freedom. This man's story in dialogue with the scripture, the liturgy and the church's teaching on discipleship fostered a conversation about how costly it can sometimes be to live the life we are called to live. The candidate went home that day with the resolve to be more loving. He asked for the gift of patience and the ability to endure, while his troubles remain with him.

It is important that catechists keep in contact with one another throughout the month and from week to week. Catechists communicate with each other in order to keep in touch with the lives of the candidates and to see if there are any issues that need to be carried over into the next week's conversation.

In some parishes, two catechists work together. One catechist serves as the primary catechist and the other catechist assists. The assisting catechist then becomes the primary catechist the following week. Adaptations are made according to the needs of the parish, candidates and catechumenal ministers. When the candidates evaluate the process, they consistently remark how they appreciated having multiple catechists. They feel that it exposes them to different perspectives and personalities. Continuity is maintained by the candidates' weekly participation and by pastoral care given to the candidates. The candidates form bonds of friendship with one another as they share their lives in the context of liturgy and the scriptures.

Those who are concerned that all Catholic dogmas and precepts are covered and who wonder how that happens in the model suggested above should be assured, that in one complete liturgical cycle, all the appropriate issues of Catholic faith and life are covered. (See Appendix I for the article "Doctrine and the Catechumenate" for further elaboration on this issue.)

In a rural or college setting, adaptations would be made accordingly. Perhaps in a rural setting families could be prepared to invite a catechumen or candidate into their home, and with some help, share the word with them. There are many resources available to assist in such endeavors.[6] The needs, available resources and, above all, the imagination of a given community determine the shape of the catechumenate. There is no one right way. If the parish is attentive to the principles of the RCIA and if the adaptation works for the parish, then it is right for that parish. The text very wisely does not give a recipe. It simply points the way and sets forth principles. It is up to the practitioners to adapt it in the parish.

If initiation belongs to all the baptized, then all the baptized must be capable of doing it. The gifts for catechumenal ministry are present in every community, no matter the size of that community. The task is to uncover those gifts. With a little creativity and tenacity it is amazing how those gifts manage to turn up in the most obscure places. Sometimes our programmatic mindsets blind us to possibilities; we see catechumenal ministry only in terms of organized, formal ministry. While that is certainly one model, even the smallest ministry settings have within them the seeds of catechumenal formation.

Parishioners who reach out to the poor and minister to the sick, for example, are certainly able to share their ministry with someone preparing for initiation. With a little direction, they could easily place their ministry within the context of the church's teaching on social justice, paschal mystery, healing, ministry and discipleship. Parishes need to find the best way to pass on the tradition in their particular circumstances, whether that be around a kitchen table, a soup kitchen or a fence on the south forty. No matter what limitations face a parish or ministry setting, the key is not to see the limitations, but the possibilities. When a parish does not fit the model of a large, urban, middle-class parish, it is important that it does not try to clone itself after that model.

The people in each setting must discover the charisms within their own community and capitalize on those gifts when trying to implement the rite. The people who minister in those settings know their unique situations. The only way to adapt the rite according to their own particular needs is to have the principles of the RCIA indelibly imprinted on their hearts. Only when they are at home with the rite will they be able to adapt it to work in their setting.

PARISHIONERS

Candidates for initiation learn how to pray because of the parishioners who pray and celebrate the liturgy of the word with them week after week. They learn how to live the Beatitudes by walking with the parishioners who live them. Some parishioners may participate in the actual process of initiation by simply lending their support. They may attend sessions as members of the faithful who just want to offer their prayer, support and encouragement to the candidates.

Other parishioners may have other roles as well. One lady in our parish coordinates the parish ministries for the catechumenate. She invites representatives from all the outreach programs to come and share their ministry with the candidates for initiation. The ministry representatives then invite the candidates to participate in their respective ministries. Other parishioners participate in the catechumenate when asked to come and witness to some aspect of their Catholic faith and life. Others serve as ministers of hospitality, providing coffee and doughnuts when requested.

In general, the parishioners are so tuned in to the folks preparing for initiation that the candidates tell stories of being stopped by parishioners at grocery stories, doctor's offices and at the mall to offer support and encouragement. They tell stories of parishioners offering their hand of encouragement as the candidates process out with their catechist for breaking open the word. The community's effect on the candidates is immeasurable.

SPONSORS

The role of the sponsor officially begins with the period of the catechumenate and lasts until the Rite of Election, at which time the unbaptized choose godparents. (The sponsor may be chosen to fulfill the role of godparent, but should not expect that this would always be the case.) Some parishes have the sponsor begin with the candidate from the very beginning of the inquiry period. Other parishes wait until a short time before the Rite of Acceptance is celebrated. There is no hard and fast rule that the role of the sponsor ends with election. It is simply the time for the godparents to emerge, if different from the sponsor.

The sponsor is the candidate's link to the parish. It is the sponsor's role to help incorporate the candidate into the life of the community. When there is outreach or spiritual activity occurring in the parish, it is the sponsor's role to inform and invite the candidate to participate. The sponsor maintains contact during the week to see how things are going in the life of the candidate, to answer questions and to share how the liturgy from Sunday continues to impact his or her life throughout the week. The sponsor is not an expert; her or she is simply a companion and thus should be willing to say, "I do not know the answer, but I will find out." The sponsor introduces the candidate to other parishioners; to some of the details of the liturgy, such as postures and gestures; and to some of our other practices of prayer, such as the rosary and the Liturgy of the Hours. The sponsor invites the candidate to accompany him or her on missions of outreach, evangelization or any other gospel-centered activity. A sponsor is hospitable, available, flexible, respectful, compassionate, open, honest, realistic, prayerful and able to listen. He or she is a confidant who respects confidentiality and is respectful of the previous religious history of the candidate, avoiding any attitude of triumphalism.

Sponsors have a key role in the area of discernment. They witness to the moral character and development of the candidate and attest to the candidate's intention to go forward for the sacraments of initiation. Sponsors assist the candidates in moments of doubt and hesitancy (RCIA, 10, 11).

At the Rite of Election, the godparent, on behalf of the church, witnesses that the candidate is ready to go forward for the Easter sacraments (RCIA, 11). The godparent attests that he or she has witnessed, by word and deed, that this candidate is truly ready for the sacraments of initiation—that adherence to the gospel and the church has indeed taken place (#131).

The sponsor and godparent are integral to the ongoing process of discernment. As they journey with the candidates week after week, they are privileged to witness the metanoia that gradually unfolds in their lives. More than anyone, the sponsor is aware when connections are not being made and when there are areas where growth is still needed. While respectful of the confidentiality they share with their candidate, sponsors can help catechists address their candidate's needs by suggesting areas that need attention.

DIRECTOR

Although the RCIA never mentions a director of initiation, there is a need for someone (or a group of someones) to administer and manage the process. Someone must interview the candidates when they come knocking, hear their stories and discern how to best address their formation needs. Someone must start the record-keeping process and determine whether the person is a candidate for baptism or for the completion of initiation sacraments. Someone must be attentive to the situation of candidates who need annulments and monitor the progress of those often-lengthy processes. Someone must be responsible for knowing how the candidates are progressing and for being attentive to them throughout the process. A continuous catechumenate requires that pastoral care be given primary consideration. The director very often is in the best position to assume this role. However, the role of director may also be a shared role within the initiation ministry. Whether one person assumes the role or whether it is a shared ministry, some one person should have frequent conversations or interviews with the candidates; this is a necessary component in their ongoing formation.

Let me offer an example: In my parish, it was mistakenly discerned that a candidate belonged in the precatechumenate for a period of time. For some reason, this woman's previous formation and religious background was not fully understood. She not only did not belong in the precatechumenate, she would ultimately be in the catechumenate for a brief period. When she was called to see how things were going for her, she intimated that she was thinking of leaving the process; it was just not for her. After an extended conversation, it became apparent that the experience was just too elementary for her; she was already evangelized. She was looking for something more and did not feel that she was getting it in the period of evangelization. A Rite of Welcome was celebrated and she moved immediately into the period of the catechumenate. That solved her dilemma and provided the depth she was seeking. Unless that contact had been made, she might have left the process, and no one would have been the wiser. It was a lesson for us to be more thorough in our initial discernment with candidates. It is amazing how much a parish can learn about initiation ministry through the mistakes it makes.

PRIEST

The pastor is responsible for the pastoral care of the catechumens and candidates. The pastor maintains a friendly relationship with the candidates and assures them of his continued pastoral care and support. The candidates understand that his pastoral responsibilities include care of them as well as the other members of the parish. Thus, the pastor encourages the candidates to approach him with their concerns. The pastor should periodically inquire as to the progress of the catechumens and candidates and offer encouragement, a listening ear and prayer support, "especially to those who seem hesitant or discouraged" (RCIA, 13). The priest also approves of the choice of godparents.

The priest, or another delegated priest, presides at the celebration of baptism, confirmation and eucharist. He also presides at most of the other liturgical rites, particularly those taking place at Sunday liturgy. Certain minor rites (blessings and minor exorcisms) may be presided over by a deacon or catechist, as well as by a priest. The priest may at times share the responsibility as catechist.

DEACON

The deacon also may assist in the catechumenate. It is enjoined upon the deacon to minister to the pastoral needs of catechumens and candidates and to assist where needed in the implementation of the rite. Thus, deacons as well as priests share in the pastoral care of the catechumens and candidates. They often serve in multiple roles in the process. The deacon encourages the candidates to approach him with their spiritual concerns and is available to them for pastoral care when needed. In addition to offering pastoral care, the deacon often assists in the ministry of catechesis (RCIA, 13). The deacon may also preside over many of the liturgical rites of the catechumenate, such as the Rite of Acceptance, celebrations of the word of God, minor rites, anointing of catechumens, the scrutinies as well as the preparatory rites.

SUMMARY PRINCIPLES FOR THE PERIOD OF THE CATECHUMENATE

Throughout this chapter, many principles of this period have been enumerated. Let us summarize them here:

—Uncatechized, unbaptized persons are in the period of the catechumenate for at least one complete liturgical cycle from the celebration of the Rite of Acceptance until their initiation at the Easter Vigil a year later.

—Uncatechized, baptized persons are in the period of the catechumenate for a period of time that parallels the time spent by catechumens.

—Baptized persons who are somewhat catechized are in the period of the catechumenate for as long as necessary to complete their Christian formation. A Rite of Reception is celebrated at the Sunday liturgy when it is discerned they are ready to come into full communion of the Catholic church.

—Baptized, fully catechized persons are given a period of sacramental preparation. When the brief period of sacramental preparation is completed, they are received into the full communion of the Catholic church at the Sunday liturgy.

—Fully catechized, unbaptized persons may be fully initiated under the provisions provided in Christian Initiation of Adults in Exceptional Circumstances (RCIA, part 2, section 3). However, unless an undue hardship or an extended period of time would result in waiting for participation in the Easter Vigil, such persons would benefit from taking part in the period of purification and enlightenment and the Easter Vigil.

—Active Catholics who were never confirmed enter a brief period of sacramental preparation for the sacrament of confirmation and then celebrate confirmation with the bishop.

—Catholics who were baptized and received their first communion but who never again put their faith into practice would benefit from an extended catechumenal-like experience. The bishop confirms such persons, unless permission is granted for the parish pastor to confirm.

MAUREEN

Our catechumen Maureen has been in the catechumenate for over a year. The change in her life is dramatic—behavior, attitude and perspective. Everyone in her life has noticed the change. The elements of catechesis mentioned above have taken deep root in Maureen's life. She is deeply involved in the life of the community. She is a member of a small Christian community. She has deep love for the word of God and obviously lives according to its principles. She serves in the St. Vincent de Paul ministry and participates in the various fundraising activities for the homeless of her city. Maureen is a mentor for at-risk elementary school children. She is responsible for inviting and bringing two coworkers to the parish—one a returning Catholic, one a baptized candidate who was deeply touched by the conversion he witnessed in Maureen and who wanted for himself what he witnessed in her.

She participates in parish retreat programs, and she treasures her weekly hour in the chapel. Maureen is ready to go forward for the Easter sacraments, and her godparent is eager to testify on her behalf. She is ready to be named an "elect of God" and to be enrolled for the sacraments of initiation at the Easter Vigil. Maureen is now ready to celebrate the Rite of Election and to enter the period of purification and enlightenment.

NOTES

1. We have since developed such a process of sacramental formation and preparation. A small team was trained to work with catechized folks from another ecclesial tradition who seek full communion into the Catholic church. This formation also extends to active Catholics who for one reason or another were never confirmed and need to be prepared for the sacrament of confirmation.

2. Some parishes celebrate children's liturgy of the word. In that case, the children are dismissed with the parish children for the liturgy of the word and then are dismissed from that liturgy to break open the word.

3. Huels, John, M. *The Catechumenate and the Law* (Chicago, Liturgy Training Publications, 1994), 17.

4. If initiation belongs to all the baptized, then the celebration of the rites of initiation need to be celebrated with the entire parish. Thus, when rites are celebrated throughout the year on an ongoing basis—that is, when there are multiple Rites of Acceptance and Welcome, and multiple Rites of Reception into the Full Communion of the Catholic Church celebrated throughout the year—they need to be celebrated at one time or another at all of the Masses in the parish community.

5. A wonderful resource on the topic of discernment is written by Donna Steffen, *Discerning Disciples,* Paulist Press, 1997.

6. *Word and Worship Workbook for Year C,* by Mary Birmingham, Paulist Press, 1998; *Word and Worship Workbook for Year A,* by Mary Birmingham, Paulist Press, 1999; *Word and Worship Workbook for Year C,* by Mary Birmingham, Paulist Press, 2000.

The Collegeville Pastoral Dictionary of Biblical Theology, Stuhlmueller, Carroll, CP, ed. The Liturgical Press, 1996.

The Word We Celebrate, Patricia Datchuck Sanchez, Sheed and Ward, 1986.

The Cultural World of Jesus, John Pilch, The Liturgical Press, 1995.

The New Dictionary of Theology, Komonchak, Joseph A., et al., eds. The Liturgical Press, 1990.

The New Dictionary of Sacramental Worship, Peter E. Fink, SJ, ed. The Liturgical Press, 1990.

CHAPTER 7

The Period of Purification and Enlightenment

Knocked breathless by the touch of the Spirit in his life, a young man named Francesco Bernadoni appeared before the bishop in the town square. To onlookers his appearance suggested that he was mad. He railed against the power, privilege and wealth of the church. Francesco challenged the bishop and insisted that the church should divest itself, and to make his point, he stripped naked in front of the bishop.

How would that behavior be treated today? What would we call a college-age man who drops out of school and out of normal life to follow Jesus? This one we call Saint Francis of Assisi.

How do we know what is authentic conversion and what is bizarre behavior? It is often hard to discern correctly. And yet that is exactly what we are called to do.

The period of purification and enlightenment, which coincides with the season of Lent, is a time of retreat and interior reflection on the part of candidates, the elect and all the faithful. It is a time to look deep within and discern the areas where sin still lurks and where there is need for deep conversion. Conversion and discernment are threads that run through the entire catechumenal process. If we are called to discern the readiness of candidates for initiation, then we must understand the dynamics of discernment and conversion.

DISCERNMENT AND THE CHURCH

The *Rite of Christian Initiation of Adults* is clear on the subject of discernment: It is not optional.

> Before the rite (of acceptance) is celebrated, . . . sufficient and necessary time, as required in each case, should be set aside to evaluate and, if necessary, to purify the candidates' motives and dispositions. With the help of the sponsors, catechists, and deacons, pastors have the responsibility for judging the outward indications of such dispositions. (RCIA, 43)

> At this second step (the Rite of Election), on the basis of the testimony of godparents and catechists and of the catechumens' reaffirmation of their intention, the Church judges their state of readiness and decides on their advancement toward the sacraments of initiation. Thus the Church makes its "election," that is, the choice and admission of those catechumens who have the dispositions that make them fit to take part . . . in the sacraments of initiation. (#119)

The RCIA insists that discernment belongs to the church. It is the responsibility of the church to judge the authenticity, maturity and adequacy of conversion. As ministers of initiation we need to know what to look for. Just what does this conversion look like?

The Sundays of Lent, in particular, invite us to embark on a journey of deep conversion. In modern usage, conversion often refers to an event, "a singular experience of being born again in Jesus Christ on a given occasion. It entails becoming a Christian and being saved on a given occasion."[1] This narrow vision helps those who go through such a one-time event to distance themselves from the imperative of continuous conversion. "It is usually 'other people' who need to heed the message. It is seldom directed inwardly to ourselves and even less to a call to societal or ecclesial change."[2] To understand conversion as a Catholic concept, we must begin with our Catholic roots, scripture and tradition, particularly as it is transmitted in the documents and rites of the church.

SCRIPTURE

Ronald Wintherup asserts that the scriptural perspective of conversion involves some form of change.[3] It is fluid, moving and dynamic. When the Old Testament refers to the human person it means a united wholeness. The human being of our Hebrew ancestors is not separated into body and spirit, as in later Greek anthropology. The perspective of conversion in the scriptures involves the action of the whole person—body, mind and spirit. One in need of conversion is someone who is in dire need of a change in the direction of his or her life. So great is their need that they are to halt dead in their tracks, make an about-face and move in the opposite direction from their original course. Conversion is a big change, a monumental change!

The Old Testament speaks not only of human conversion, but also of the conversion of God. How presumptuous this seems to us! Is God in need of conversion? Not at all. Yet the God of the Old Testament repeatedly changes course. This is always done as an act of love and repentance. "If you remain quietly in this land I will build you up, and not tear you down; I will plant you, not uproot you; for I regret the evil I have done you" (Jeremiah 42:10). "From the [Old Testament] perspective, then, God is a God of change and of integrity, one who can set limits on relating to the world and yet who can also have a change of heart when deemed appropriate."[4] God gives us the perfect model of conversion and repentance. If God can have a change of heart, then, we can do no less. Repentance can only be accomplished through the grace of God. Human beings, left to their own designs, are incapable of true repentance. God will accomplish the repentance of his people by divine initiative, not human design.

In the Old Testament, symbolic gestures and rituals often accompany conversion.[5] The most observable ritual is ritual cleansing, also prominent in the New Testament. Ezekiel's proclamation of God sprinkling clean water upon Israel while offering a new heart in place of Israel's stony heart is indicative of Israel's ritual celebration of God's covenant and the ongoing journey of conversion with the people of God.

The New Testament understands conversion in terms of *metanoia* (change in one's mind and direction) and *epistrepho* (change in direction, a turning away from or toward). Conversion presupposes remorse for one's actions and is an act of repentance. As in the Old Testament, conversion involves a change in one's life and turning toward God. "Conversion is a process rather than a once-for-all-time action."[6]

Both Testaments speak definitively on the issue of conversion. It is not a one-time event. It is always a movement either toward something or away from something. The primary perspective of the New Testament is turning away from sin and turning toward God and Jesus.

Conversion in the gospel of Matthew picks up a theme that appears in Mark: Conversion goes hand in hand with faith and discipleship. Matthew, however, nuances it further. He connects conversion with "bearing good fruit." True conversion will be evidenced in the fruit that it bears. From Matthew's perspective, "people reap exactly what they sow. Matthew has a great concern that interior motivation be matched by exterior reality."[7]

Matthew insists that conversion requires an ethical response. It involves a personal choice with attached consequences. Conversion leads to salvation. Matthew ultimately embraces scripture's common understanding of conversion—turning away from sin and foolishness, and turning toward God and new life.

Luke personalizes conversion. Rather than simply a call to the people or the nation, as in the Old Testament, conversion for Luke is individual. His understanding of conversion is based in the mercy of God. "For Luke, conversion and repentance, forgiveness and reconciliation, are all a part of the 'wideness of God's mercy.'"[8] Luke's concept of conversion, reconciliation and the mercy of God is the basis for our understanding of the sacrament of reconciliation. Rather than an extended meditation on sin, the sacrament celebrates the fount of grace at the hands of our merciful God.

CHURCH DOCUMENTS

The *Constitution on the Sacred Liturgy* understands conversion as a call to faith in Jesus Christ. The Decree on the Church's Missionary Activity asserts that conversion involves awareness of being delivered from sin and led into the mystery of God's love and a personal relationship with him (CSL, 13). The decree understands conversion as a spiritual journey, a process in which a person gradually and progressively changes. Following the lead of scripture, the church understands conversion as a process, a journey, a change in outlook, behavior and life. "When man accepts the Spirit of Christ, he establishes a *way of life* that is totally new and gratuitous."[9] Conversion is a turning toward or a return to God with our whole being. Conversion desires an end to sin and is a turning away from evil, "with repugnance toward the evil actions we have committed."[10] Conversion involves the commitment to change one's life, while trusting in the grace and mercy of God to accomplish the task.[11]

RITE OF CHRISTIAN INITIATION OF ADULTS

For those of us who work in Christian initiation, the *Rite of Christian Initiation of Adults* is our guide to conversion. The rite's view of conversion can be summarized by six points.

First, conversion is an entrance into a covenant. This is biblical language. God entered into a covenant with the human race. At the creation of the world God entered into a reciprocal covenant with the human race. God promised and still promises to love, nurture and care for men and women. It is a gift freely given, and is always initiated by God. In response to this incredible, gratuitous gift, men and women would love the Lord their God with their entire heart, mind and soul. As evidence of that love, they would love one another, care for those who could not care for themselves, and be good stewards of the earth. As one reads the language of the rite, the initiation process invites people into that committed, reciprocal covenant with God.

Second, conversion is centered in Christ—his life, death, resurrection, ascension and sending of the Spirit. That does not mean that everyone who begins the process will already have Christ at their center. John arrived on the doorstep to say, "I am in love with Sarah. She is a Catholic. She wants to marry a Catholic boy. I'm not Catholic, but I love Sarah. So here I am. I'm open. Teach me." Two years later, John was baptized. Another young man, a Buddhist who had absolutely no sense of Jesus whatsoever, was asked what brought him to the process. He responded, "My wife is a Catholic, and she says I have to." Spilling over with emotion, he could not contain himself during the Holy Saturday morning preparation rites. With volcanic force, his words erupted midst the gathered assembly: "I love Jesus so much!" The words were simple, yet a mighty reflection of the deep, intense metanoia experienced by this young man.

Many people are attracted to our tradition for various reasons, not all having to do with Jesus Christ. No matter what the catalyst for those first stirrings of faith, ultimately an authentic, mature conversion demands that Christ be the center. Anything else at the center is idolatry. Papal authority or a particular way of reading scripture is very attractive to some people. That is all well and good. However, if those things are at the center, conversion is flawed.

Third, conversion is ecclesial. Conversion is of the church and within the church. Conversion is not a "Jesus and me" affair. It is not private. Conversion is public and communal. It takes place within and in the midst of the church. This is a difficult concept for modern-day people, especially Americans. Many ministers of initiation have experienced resistance from people when it comes to celebrating public rites. This is a product of American obsession with privacy and rugged individualism.

Peter told the director, "I am a very private person. I have waited a long time before coming to you because I refuse to get up in front of the public." The director pleaded with Peter, "Just trust us, we'll work with you." After Peter's very public celebration of full communion, he responded, "I have come to see that celebrating the important moments of my life have deep meaning. In celebrating the rites with this community, it reinforced my decision and commitment. I guess this really isn't just about God and me, is it?"

Catholic conversion needs to unfold gradually in the midst of the Body of Christ, who is present in the community and in a church that is bold enough to proclaim, "If you want to touch Christ, look around the assembly because that is where you will find him." If you are not comfortable embracing Christ in the people, then you are not comfortable embracing Christ.

Fourth, conversion is a sacramental experience. This is understood on two levels.

Conversion is something that is incarnated; it finds expression in flesh. It is not just a spiritual reality. Conversion has a shape, a feel, a touch. It is experienced in the senses. Conversion also is celebrated and nurtured in ritual activity. Our entire sacramental system is about conversion. So much of this is this true, that we could say that anyone whose conversion has not been sacramentalized is a person whose conversion is not complete.

Lewis Rambo cites the work of sociologist Virginia Hines regarding the place ritual plays in the process of religious conversion:

> Commitment rituals are bridge-burning events, effective because they serve three functions. First the convert enacts the ritual ceremony and thus embodies the transformation process. Dramatizing change, acting out a role is more effective than merely talking about change. A public proclamation of the rejection of an old way of life, however subtle or implicit and embracing of the new, consolidates the conversion

process. Hines asserts that the bridge-burning rituals of conversion provide the individual with powerful subjective experiences that confirm the beliefs of the group and transform the convert's self image. New members are ritually reaffirmed in their convictions.[12]

This is why the rites of initiation are not optional. It matters a great deal when parishes choose not to celebrate the scrutinies. When we celebrate the sacred mysteries, we encounter God in fullness. Sacraments "not only presuppose faith, but by words and objects they also nourish, strengthen and express it. . . . They do indeed impart grace, but, in addition, the very act of celebrating them disposes the faithful most effectively to receive this grace in a fruitful manner, to worship God duly and to practice charity."[13] In other words, sacramental celebrations dispose people to conversion! We bear a heavy weight of responsibility when we choose to celebrate our rites minimally.

One woman named Dorothy shared her experience of the scrutiny: "When Father laid hands on me, and the community prayed with me, I could feel the weight of my hatred for a very difficult relative, a hatred that consumed me and got in the way of my relationship with God. The hatred finally melted away. Alone I seemed powerless, now I think with God's help I can let it go. Gosh, it almost felt like an exorcism—so much garbage is gone!"

Fifth, conversion is a spiritual journey, to use a metaphor from scripture. It is a journey fraught with ups and downs, highs and lows, two steps forward, one step back. There will be shifts and movements throughout the catechumenate. Sometimes someone has to go down to the ashes in order to rise up like a phoenix. We have to experience sin and failure to know what grace is really all about. That is why we sing the Exsultet at the Easter Vigil, "O happy fault, O necessary sin of Adam." We do not judge or condemn when catechumens fail, we look at it as a moment to encounter the incredible mercy of God. This journey is lifelong.

Finally, conversion is a comprehensive transformation. The entire person undergoes a radical transformation and change. A woman commented about how a coworker is an entirely different person since he made the decision to enter the process of initiation. She affirmed that all the people in her department have noticed his transformation. So many areas of his life were affected—behavior, ways of relating to others, priorities and decision-making. Authentic conversion spills over into all areas of a person's life. "Putting on that new garment" truly embodies the reality; the newly initiated have become a new creation in Christ.

DISCERNING CONVERSION FOR ELECTION

The rite gives us some very practical ways to look at conversion, particularly for those times when we are called upon to make explicit judgment. The discernment criteria for the Rite of Acceptance were discussed in chapter 5. We are given similar criteria for the Rite of Election. Paragraph 120 of the rite insists that the elect are to have undergone a conversion in mind and action. Catechumens are to have developed a sufficient acquaintance with Christian teaching as well as adopted a spirit of charity.

There is a difference between readiness for the Rite of Acceptance and readiness for the Rite of Election. The Rite of Acceptance assumes a beginning relationship with Jesus Christ—conversion to Christ. By the time a person is ready to celebrate the Rite of Election, and thus to go forward for the Easter sacraments, this relationship should have taken deep root within the candidate for initiation. The difference, then, between discernment for acceptance and for election is conversion and adherence to the church. The criteria assumed for the celebration of this rite assumes that the person is immersed in the life of the community. He or she has embraced the Christian life within the Catholic communion. There is evidence in word and action that this conversion is deep and lasting. The church gives witness to this observed metanoia.

One need only look to paragraph 75 to see what the candidates should have been busied about throughout the period of the catechumenate. Discernment is specific to the rites, but it is also ongoing. Catechumenal ministers must listen attentively for the cues and for evidence of the conversion that is taking place in the lives of the candidates; they must also affirm that evidence when it is observed. Discernment takes place through dialogue, conversation, storytelling and prayer throughout the entire process of initiation. If we are asking the "so what" questions during the catechumenate, and listening to the answers, discernment is taking place all the time.

DISCERNMENT AND CONVERSION

Discernment and conversion are not only the tasks of catechumens, candidates and the elect, but also the tasks and responsibility of the entire church.

Ann was an angry, bitter woman. She was hunched over; life had been hard on her. She was faithful in coming to the initiation sessions, but conversion was slow. All she could see was how life had dealt her a bitter hand. But as people reached out to her and showed her unconditional love she started to change. Conversion was gradual. At first, it was evident in her ability to stand upright and smile. Slowly she started to talk about God, then about her responsibility to other people. Ann started to help out in parish outreach. She bought an entire wardrobe for a poor family. Yet by the time Lent arrived, even though her conversion was radical, it was not complete.

Ann celebrated the first scrutiny, but she was uncomfortable. At the second, she became increasing agitated. Finally, the dam burst. It was something she had been harboring all through the process—all through her life. She was too ashamed to tell anyone. She refused to tell anyone. It was an obstacle and she knew it. She refused to let go. Yet Ann knew she could never go forward for initiation if she didn't let go. At the final scrutiny she experienced freedom, and she shared her freedom with the parish community.

She grew up in a bigoted home. Part of her family experience was rooted in hatred for African Americans. It is what she knew. She saw nothing wrong with her family's bigotry. She was raised in it. No matter how often we talked about our responsibility to others, how we are to love one another and cast aside our hatred, it never applied to her bigotry. She was comfortable with it. Radical change occurred in her life in every area of her life except one, this one. In time, though, she knew that there was something lurking within her that was just not right. Her angst grew with each preparation session and each celebration of the scrutinies. She was gently urged to confront the blind demon that was responsible for the climate of hate that enveloped her in her formative years.

She knew that to turn away from this evil meant she would no longer be welcome in her family. Coming to that awareness was a very difficult moment in this woman's life. It was almost more painful than making the decision to change. Once she named her sin and the corporate sin of her family, she knew she had to change course. She made this decision with the love, prayers and support of the Christian community. She ritualized her decision when she celebrated the scrutinies in the parish community.

Like an onion whose layers were peeled away one sheath at a time, this woman's conversion was slow, gradual and took place within a loving, albeit challenging community. Discernment is ongoing. It takes place through continuous reflection and dialogue with the scriptures and through active, reflective listening on the part of catechists and the community. When the gospel invites a radical response and a challenge to turn away from sinful behaviors, one need only listen to the candidates' response and observe the subsequent action in his or her life to determine if conversion is indeed taking place.

The period of purification and enlightenment provided the fertile environment for Ann to confront the demon that had taken up residence in her family's consciousness. It also provided the means to be delivered from it—the scrutinies.

A HISTORICAL PERSPECTIVE ON PURIFICATION AND ENLIGHTENMENT

The period of purification and enlightenment is patterned after the way that people were prepared for initiation in the early church. In the first and second century it was a time of intense prayer and fasting. The catechumens, the candidates and the community prayed for deliverance.

Originally Lent was a period of fasting in preparation for celebrating the paschal vigil. By the middle of the fourth century, Lent was a 40-day period of fasting and preparation for the Easter Triduum, which included baptism. The whole church fasted and prayed in solidarity with those preparing for baptism.

> Christians saw in fasting a way of preparing for the reception of the Spirit, a powerful weapon in the fight against evil spirits, an appropriate preparation for the reception of baptism and the eucharist and a way of being able to help the poor with money that would otherwise have been spent on food. What the church required of candidates for baptism by way of liturgical and spiritual effort was also done by the faithful in solidarity of spirit. An atmosphere of cooperation and reciprocity was thus established that benefited the entire community.[14]

Every morning the catechumens were prayed over at Mass, and they spent three hours a day in prayer. The scrutinies were held on the third, fourth and fifth Sundays of Lent. The gospel readings for those Sundays were the encounter of Jesus with the Samaritan woman, the healing of the man born blind and the raising of Lazarus.

By the fifth century there was the first major development in the Roman observance of Lent. The penitential nature of Lent began to take precedence and the baptismal focus receded. The focus on fasting and repentance predominated, and the number of candidates for adult initiation declined. Infant baptism became the almost exclusive practice of initiation. The rites associated with preparation of the elect began to disappear or be radically transformed. The readings for the scrutinies were moved to weekdays. Much of the original meaning and understanding of Lent disappeared.

Not until the Second Vatican Council was the original understanding and practice of Lent restored. The *Constitution on the Sacred Liturgy* affirms that the season of Lent has a twofold character; it is a time for recalling or preparing for baptism, and for penance. In this way the entire church prepares to celebrate the paschal mystery of Jesus Christ at the Easter Vigil and throughout the season (CSL, 109). This early understanding of Lent was restored through liturgies, homilies and catechesis that emphasized the twofold nature of the season. It was also accomplished by the celebration of the scrutinies/exorcism and presentation of the Lord's Prayer and Creed that is the hallmark of this period of conversion and discernment.

The restored vision of Lent sees it as the period in which the elect and church reflect on the mystery of sin in all its sinister forms—personal, social and systemic—and seek deliverance from Christ, the liberator. The question for discernment and conversion is, What still needs to change in the elect before they enter into this new life? As the entire community ponders this question, they also ask, What needs to change in us so that we can more fully commit ourselves to this life?

THE PERIOD OF PURIFICATION AND ENLIGHTENMENT

The RCIA reminds us that the period of purification and enlightenment is preparation for celebration of paschal mystery (RCIA, 138). The elect and the community are purified during this season in order to enter more fully into the paschal mystery that is remembered and made present most especially at the Easter Vigil.

Lent is a time of retreat and reflection. This period of purification and enlightenment looks at the ugliness of sin at its core—its enormity, its allure, its power to destroy lives. The mind and heart are purified, and the conscience is probed. The elect and the faithful are called to do penance as they prepare for the celebration of baptism for the elect and renewal of baptismal promises for the faithful (RCIA, 139).

The primary lens of this period is conversion and discernment. The rites of this period seek to probe the need for healing and transformation that still exists in the elect, in preparation for baptism. The elect will reject evil at their baptism, and the scrutinies prepare them to make that rejection. The scrutinies foreshadow a lifetime of celebrating the sacrament of reconciliation.

The presentations of Lent prepare the elect for baptism and eucharist. The Presentation of the Creed prepares them to make their profession of faith; the Presentation of the Lord's Prayer prepares the elect for becoming adopted children of God through baptism. Just as the Lord's Prayer prepares the community for the reception of eucharist at every liturgy, so too does it prepare the elect for the reception of their first communion and their ongoing life in the eucharistic community.

Just as in the early church, the entire community joins the elect in solidarity and prayer. The enlightenment of Lent imbues the elect and the faithful with a more intimate knowledge of Christ, who liberates the world from sin and evil. Lent is a time of retreat and intense spiritual reflection and preparation. It is not a time for further instruction.

Of all the strange-sounding names in the RCIA, none is more strange than *scrutiny*. Many people think that the verb *scrutinize* has negative overtones: to investigate, or to uncover something that is less than desirable. The word *scrutiny* comes from a Greek word that means "to look deeply into." The elect look deeply into those areas still in need of the healing, liberating touch of Christ. Only the unbaptized celebrate the scrutinies. Baptized candidates have already experienced this deliverance from evil at their baptism. Candidates join the community in the preparation for the scrutinies and then take their rightful place with the baptized when these rites are celebrated with the elect. The RCIA provides an optional penitential rite for baptized candidates similar to the scrutiny. This rite may be celebrated on the Second Sunday of Lent.

IMPLEMENTING THE PERIOD OF PURIFICATION AND ENLIGHTENMENT

What, then, takes place in this period? The elect, adults and children, continue to gather with the Sunday assembly. They continue to be dismissed for breaking open the word. The elect gather with the community for the parish lenten renewal and retreat experiences. They enter into mystagogical reflection on the celebration of the Rite of Election. The elect prepare for the celebration of the scrutinies. Following the celebration of each scrutiny they enter into mystagogical reflection on the experience.

During the period of purification and enlightenment the elect prepare for and celebrate the presentations of the Creed and the Lord's Prayer. They prepare for and gather with the community for the celebration of the Triduum liturgies. They are dismissed from the Holy Thursday and Good Friday liturgies and participate in the Holy Saturday preparation rites. After a year of dismissal catechesis, the elect are so accustomed to breaking open the scriptures, that with some preparatory assistance they are often capable of leading and entering into reflection on the scriptures of Holy Thursday and Good Friday without the leadership of the catechist. In so doing, the catechist is freed to celebrate those liturgies with the parish community.

Yet it is important to note that it may not always be pastorally advisable to dismiss the elect without a catechist. Regardless of whether a catechist facilitates the session or not, a leader is needed. One of the elect could be prepared to lead a reflection on the liturgy of the word. However, there may not always be someone with the necessary skills to do so. In that case a decision would need to be made to either have the elect remain for the rest of the liturgy or invite a catechist to make the necessary sacrifice to facilitate the dismissal catechesis. In the event that the decision is made that the elect remain for the rest of the liturgy, it might be appropriate to gather for a brief period of reflection following the celebration.

Keeping in mind the vision of the year-round, ongoing catechumenate, there will likely be catechumens who will not be initiated at the Easter Vigil and who are still in process. Some catechumens may have only recently celebrated a Rite of Acceptance and thus would not be initiated until the following year. They would not necessarily or intentionally be invited to participate in the Triduum liturgies. However, if they are in attendance, they may be dismissed with the elect, dismissed to their homes or remain in the assembly.

The path of the already baptized, while similar, is nonetheless distinct. They, too, gather on Sunday with the community. They, too, participate in the parish retreat and renewal experiences. The baptized candidates prepare for, celebrate and reflect upon the celebration of the call to continuing conversion. They and the community are invited to participate in the preparation for, celebration of and reflection on the scrutinies; they also prepare for and are invited to celebrate the sacrament of reconciliation. Finally, they participate in the liturgies of the Triduum as well as the preparation activities for the Rite of Reception into Full Communion.

THE WEEKS OF LENT

First Week. Since Lent is a time of retreat, the environment and gatherings for the elect should convey that change in tone and atmosphere. Where once the group met in a room on the parish campus, perhaps they might now meet in the church for the period of Lent. If the group meets in another space, the environment should reflect the season. Each session begins with the liturgy of the word.

As the elect gather for the first time after the celebration of the Rite of Sending for Election and the Rite of Election, they are eager to examine the experience. The liturgies, scriptures, homilies, ritual actions, symbols and gestures are remembered, both from a personal and ecclesial perspective. They share how the experience touched them and provided meaning for their lives. They reflect on how the liturgies revealed the presence and action of God. They meditate on what it means to be chosen by God. The elect remember the symbols of the rite, what they expressed and revealed, and how they provide meaning for the elect's lives.

Second Week. The elect and candidates gather during the week to prepare for full, conscious and active participation in the scrutinies that will be celebrated on the Third Sunday of Lent. Preparation does not mean rehearsal. Preparation involves heightening their awareness to encounter more fully the mysteries inherent in the rites. Thus, the elect, candidates and faithful gather to reflect on the mystery of sin so that the enormity of that reality may be brought to the celebration of the scrutiny, perhaps asking, Where in our lives and in our culture are we parched from the effects of sin? One or more of the scripture readings from the scrutiny are brought to bear on that reflection. The elect and those gathered tune their minds and hearts to encounter the liberation of Christ in the celebration of the scrutiny that will take place on Sunday.

As part of their lenten formation, some of the catechumens and candidates who will not be initiated at the Easter Vigil may be invited along with the community to participate in the spiritual preparation sessions for the scrutinies. As members of the assembly they would experience the scrutiny at the Sunday liturgy. It therefore makes sense to prepare them to enter fully and consciously into the experience. This would not necessarily be advisable for someone who is new to the catechumenate. He or she might need more time in formation before jumping headlong into what can sometimes be an intense reflection on the nature of grace and sin in our lives and in the world. Perhaps such persons would need a gradual immersion into such issues that further time in the catechumenate would afford. As always, careful discernment is needed.

Third and Fourth Weeks of Lent. The presentation of the Creed takes place the week following the celebration of the first scrutiny, perhaps when the elect and candidates gather for the liturgy of the word, unless the presentations were anticipated during the period of the catechumenate (RCIA, 147). They also engage in mystagogical reflection on the celebration of the first scrutiny and prepare for the celebration of the next one. Using images from the scriptures for the coming Sunday, they prepare for the next scrutiny. They allow the word of God and the celebration of the scrutinies to lead them deeper in their quest for healing, purification and enlightenment. They open their lives to the ongoing transforming power of the risen Christ.

Fifth Week. The Presentation of the Lord's Prayer takes place during the fifth week, after the celebration of the third scrutiny, unless it is deferred for inclusion in the Holy Saturday preparation rites (RCIA, 149). The elect reflect upon the celebration of the third scrutiny. They marvel at the ways Christ has freed them from the power of evil, and they prepare for the liturgies of Holy Week.

Holy Week. The elect anticipate the vigil. They are prepared to encounter the symbols of the Triduum. It is a time to reflect on the cycle of death and resurrection in our lives and our participation in the paschal mystery as we approach the celebration that most fully remembers and makes present that mystery.

Triduum. The elect celebrate the liturgies of the Triduum, Mass of the Lord's Supper, Celebration of the Lord's Passion, Good Friday and Holy Saturday Morning Prayer, Holy Saturday preparation rites, and the Easter Vigil. In some parishes the neophytes participate in the Easter Sunday Masses and finally in Sunday Evening Prayer, which brings the Triduum to a close.

GODPARENTS AND SPONSORS

Godparents participate in the preparation and celebration of the lenten rituals with the elect. In the event that the godparent does not live in the same city, the sponsor continues to journey with the elect during Lent. Sponsors of baptized candidates also participate with their candidate in the penitential and baptismal preparation of Lent.

CATECHISTS

Catechists who usually serve during the period of the catechumenate might share the facilitation of the period of purification and enlightenment, although it is important to remember that in an ongoing catechumenate there are still catechumens who have not become elect. Thus, catechists are needed to facilitate the catechumenate as well as the period of purification and enlightenment. Creativity is required to attend to the needs of both. In a situation in which there is a limited number of catechists, one catechist might agree to be the catechist for the catechumens during Lent. The other catechist would minister to the elect. In a larger setting, one or two catechists could be formed to lead the period of purification and enlightenment; that would be their ministry. In such an instance the catechist(s) would participate in the regular catechumenate sessions for a period of time prior to Lent in order to become familiar with the candidates for initiation. That catechist(s) would then lead the spiritual preparation for the Rite of Election. From that point on, the catechist(s) would facilitate the lenten baptismal and penitential preparation of the elect.

Alternatively, the facilitation of the period of purification and enlightenment could be shared by various catechists as long as continuity between the sessions could be maintained. One way continuity can be achieved is to have the catechist who will be leading the next session participate in the previous one.

LITURGY PLANNERS

The primary activities of Lent are prayer, preparation for and celebration of rites. The persons responsible for liturgy planning in the parish may have an important role in the preparation and formation of the elect and baptized candidates during this season.

PARISHIONERS

Parishioners prepare for the renewal of their own baptismal promises at Easter by immersion in the season of Lent. Retreat and renewal experiences, communal celebrations of the sacrament of reconciliation and participation in the eucharist during the Sundays of Lent serve as penitential and baptismal preparation for the faithful. Parishioners may also be invited to join the elect and the candidates in the prayer and preparation sessions for the scrutinies. Parishioners pray and support the elect during this time of intense spiritual preparation.

Aidan Kavanaugh once said that a community has the energy to open the font only once a year. The implications of that statement become all too clear when one realizes the spiritual energy that is expended in preparing for baptism. We devote an entire season to prepare for it and for the renewal of our baptismal promises. It is for this reason that baptisms are primarily reserved for the night when the church seeks to generate itself, the Easter Vigil. When baptisms are celebrated according to the principles in part II of the *Rite of Christian Initiation of Adults,* Exceptional Circumstances, it is assumed that the preparatory, penitential preparation of Lent will still be provided for the candidates, including election, scrutinies and presentations. Needless to say, if baptisms were indiscriminately celebrated throughout the year, it would pose a tremendous burden on the parish. The church provides an entire season for the entire church to engage in this preparation.

MAUREEN

Maureen, our catechumen, who is now one of the elect, is ready to be fully initiated at the Easter Vigil. There are observable signs of conversion in her life. She is ready and eager to enter into the baptismal and penitential preparation of the season. Her heart is open to the ongoing transforming work of the Holy Spirit in her life. She is eager to journey with the community through this season of baptismal preparation, retreat, reflection and interior discernment. This poem expresses, perhaps, her feelings:

I thought I had uncovered it all; layer by layer I shed
it all away.
so what could be left, sister lent?
like a snake squirming from the casing
of his former self
and the butterfly wrestling from the safe bondage
of her quiet hibernation,
I stand empty,
a wonderful, curious, new creation,
chosen of God.
Nakedly I gaze before discernment's
interior mirror . . .
so what could be left, sister lent?
Sunday after Sunday, story after story,
decision after decision,

gave way to an empty, vulnerable vessel,
ready for Easter filling.
so what could be left, sister lent?
Like an air-dried sponge I stand waiting . . .
for what do I wait?
for firelight's illumination
for baptismal water's soaking immersion
for confirmation oil's sealing configuration
for eucharist bread
and wine's sumptuous celebration
for dying, for rising,
for famine, for feasting,
for those who are out to be one with the in,
to eat, to be broken, to be poured, to be filled,
to live by example, to die,
to be food for the hungry, the lost, the blind
and the obstinate.
I wait to give more of the gift already given,
the sacrament of life for the sake of the kingdom,
so forty more days of repentance and ashes
to renew, to strengthen and prepare for the banquet.
Is there more? Could there be
one forgotten remnant
of a life not yet surrendered,
of blindness, of repression?
Be it sojourn or Passover or exodus
I stand with eyes opened, my heart in my hand.
What could be left, only you know for sure,
so do what you will, root out from the core
all that might keep me from the life you intend
of thanksgiving, of service and praise till the end.[15]

NOTES

1. Witherup, Ronald D. *Conversion in the New Testament,* Collegeville: The Liturgical Press, 1994, 4.

2. Ibid, 5.

3. Ibid, 6.

4. Ibid, 14.

5. Ibid, 15.

6. Ibid, 19.

7. Ibid, 32.

8. Ibid, 56.

9. *General Catechetical Directory,* 60.

10. *Catechism of the Catholic Church,* 1431.

11. Ibid.

12. Rambo, Lewis. *Understanding Religious Conversion,* New Haven: Yale University Press, 128.

13. *Constitution on the Sacred Liturgy,* 59.

14. Adam, Adolf. *The Liturgical Year,* Collegeville, The Liturgical Press, 93.

15. Mary C. Birmingham. "Preparation for Celebration of the Scrutinies," *Christian Initiation* (February/March 1997), Kansas City: National Catholic Reporter, 1.

CHAPTER 8

Triduum

Huddled around fires, our ancient ancestors told their stories and enacted rituals that formed them into a holy nation, a consecrated assembly, a people set apart. We, too, gather this night around sacred flames to remember our origin, to tell our story and to do the business of making church. This is the night when heaven is truly wedded to earth. The Easter candle is plunged into the church's maternal waters. As she labors in love, Mother Church shouts with pangs of joy as neophytes are born and the faithful are reborn in faith.

This is the night when heavenly hosts gather around the Master's jeweled banquet table in triumphant exultation, awaiting the final communion. This is the night when Christians of earth look toward their participation in that banquet while rejoicing in the one at hand. It is sacred, earthy work. We dirty our hands in groves of olives, fields of wheat and vineyards of grapes, and we wash them again in the murky waters of life. And somehow the fruit of our labor is sanctified, transporting us into the heart of transcendent mystery.

This night is the highpoint of the premier celebration of our liturgical year, the Triduum. All the liturgies of the year point to this one great feast; it is foundational to our Catholic experience and identity. The Triduum is the mother of all feasts. It remembers and makes present the Lord's passion, death and resurrection. It is the culmination of the entire liturgical year. Lent prepares for it. The Triduum is the feast in which the church does what it was created to do—generate itself through baptizing.

The feast has its roots in Israel's saving event, the exodus, and the feast that remembers it, Passover. Christians appropriated the feast of Passover to their understanding of Jesus' own passing from death to life. Saint Augustine reminds us, "He passed through the seas of suffering and death and led the people of God to a communion of grace with the Father."

The Triduum is not merely a historical remembering; it is a remembering that makes the saving benefits of the event present. Through Jesus' saving action, the church was born and empowered to continue to give birth.

This three-day feast begins on the evening of Holy Thursday and doesn't end until the evening of Easter Sunday. The three days are marked with the Mass of the Lord's Supper, the Celebration of the Passion, the Easter Vigil and, like all days, with Morning and Evening Prayer. On Holy Saturday a special time of prayer and preparation is held with the elect. Various other types of prayer may also take place.

During this great feast we wash feet, offer gifts for the poor, venerate the cross, keep vigil, tell stories, light new fires, baptize, anoint, put on new clothes, renew baptisms, give thanks and praise, eat and drink, sing and process. All things are made new—new fire, fresh water, newly baked bread, luscious red wine. All is made new this night and revealed for what it truly is, including us.

HOLY THURSDAY AND THE ELECT

The call to service is ritualized in the liturgy of Holy Thursday with the *mandatum*, the washing of feet. This rite is particularly meaningful for the elect and candidates. It ritualizes for them the apostolic conversion that has taken place in their lives. The elect are dismissed to further reflect on the presence of Christ just encountered in word and ritual.

Dismissal during the Triduum is a question that needs some reflection. The Triduum is the night when the community gathers to celebrate what it means to be a member of the people of God. It is the night we tell the primordial family stories, eat the primordial family meal and in so doing, through the power of the Holy Spirit, bring new life into being. If ever there was a night when the church's ministers long to gather with the assembly, this is the night. Most parishes have only one celebration of the liturgies of Holy Thursday and Good Friday. Thus, if catechists were to facilitate the elect's dismissal catechesis during the Triduum, they would be absent from a good portion of the celebration. This is unnecessary. The elect are experts at breaking open the word; they have been doing it for over a year. They are more than capable of leading themselves in this very familiar activity. The disciples recognized Jesus in the breaking of the bread because it was so familiar to them. So too with the elect. Breaking open the word is so much a part of their formation that they will recognize Jesus in the breaking open of God's word, with or without the leadership of a catechist.

One of the elect in our parish is invited to facilitate the session. He or she is provided with a format, a reflection on the liturgy and a brief explanation of the scriptures. The elect break open their experience of Holy Thursday and Good Friday.

GOOD FRIDAY AND THE ELECT

The elect gather with the community for Morning Prayer. The Celebration of the Lord's Passion takes place later in the day or evening. The elect are dismissed from this liturgy, after the homily, to share the Good Friday scriptures. The intercessions and the veneration of the cross follow; the liturgy concludes with the sharing of communion. If the cross is left in place, the elect and candidates could return after the conclusion of the liturgy to venerate it. Another option would be to move the community's veneration of the cross to the end of the Good Friday liturgy so that the elect and candidates could return to venerate the cross with the assembly.

HOLY SATURDAY AND THE ELECT

Paragraph 185.1 of the RCIA maintains that the elect should refrain from usual activity and spend their time in prayer and reflection on Holy Saturday. A morning retreat in preparation for the evening celebration facilitates that prayer and reflection. While it is a day filled with anticipation and the business of getting ready for this long-awaited event, a time-out from that business helps to focus and tune the minds and the hearts of the elect on the paschal mystery they will sacramentally experience and embrace. It is time well spent. Early in Lent they are reminded that the preparatory retreat is an important part of observing the three-day feast.

The preparation rites may be celebrated in the context of such a retreat. The preparation rites prepare the candidates for full, conscious and active participation in the liturgy they will celebrate this evening and for their immersion into the paschal mystery of Christ through the celebration of the sacraments of initiation. A liturgy of the word (a format is provided at RCIA, 187–192) is celebrated in which various rites may be celebrated. The ephphetha rite impresses on the elect their need for God's strength to hear the word of God and profess it in the world. The recitation of the Creed prepares them for the profession of faith they will make before they are baptized. It also "instructs them in their duty to proclaim the message of the Gospel" (#193). If the presentation of the Creed has not been celebrated previously, it replaces the recitation of the Creed. The presentation of the Lord's Prayer, if deferred to Holy Saturday, prepares the elect to embrace their role as adopted children of God and as proximate preparation for reception of their first holy communion. While the rite includes a ritual for choosing a baptismal name, the bishops of the United States have established that it is the norm in the United States that a new name is not given; diocesan bishops may decide if it is appropriate for people coming from cultures where this is customary (RCIA, 33.5, U.S. edition).

The rite assumes that a priest or deacon is the minister of these rites (RCIA, 199). Following the liturgy, the elect, godparents and parishioners might engage in mystagogical reflection on the scriptures and the symbols of the liturgy just celebrated. Participants prayerfully reflect on the significance and the implications of the ritual that asks that the ears of the elect be opened to hear and proclaim God's word, of what it means to be an adopted child of God, and of why those rituals are preparation for the rites of initiation. The elect then might be sent home with a question that invites them to contemplate further on their imminent participation in the paschal mystery through the rites of initiation. The godparents remain for a brief period of time in order to rehearse the movements of the liturgy so they may graciously and confidently lead their candidates through the rituals.

In the event that there are baptized candidates who will be received into full Catholic communion at the Easter Vigil, they may participate in the preparatory morning retreat, prayer and reflection. However, the ephphetha and the presentations and the recitation of the Creed are celebrated only with the elect.

Catechumens who are still in the process and will not be initiated until the following year (or later) are not invited to participate in the Holy Saturday preparation rites.

EASTER VIGIL

This is the night we make the church. This is the night we celebrate our identity in the primary symbols of our faith—assembly, cross, fire, word, water, garment, oil, bread and wine. We process behind the pillar of fire just as our ancestors did when God led them out of Egypt's bondage. We are led through the darkness by the light of the Easter candle, a sign of the risen Christ, a sign of God's presence in our midst. We proclaim the primal stories of our faith and become one with those stories—we remember and make present their saving power. We follow Jesus' command to baptize all nations as we lead the elect to the waters of new life. They are immersed in the flowing waters of new life; they are baptized into the death and resurrection of Christ. If there are candidates for confirmation[1] and eucharist, they stand with the newly baptized and are slathered with the oil of the Spirit—signifying their changed reality. They are sealed with the gift of the Holy Spirit. The Holy Spirit anoints them for mission in the world. Oil, like water, is initiatory. It completes baptism and leads to eucharist. The Holy Spirit strengthens the newly initiated and the confirmandi in their role as priest, prophet and king.

The neophytes process to the table of love, sacrifice and unity—the culmination of their journey. They have been prepared for this moment. We must ask ourselves, Have we spent all our energy preparing the elect for baptism, highlighting its importance, while missing that which fully initiates them and incorporates them into the eucharistic community? Does the liturgy move with momentum and energy to this peak moment? Does the baptism overshadow the reception of eucharist? Perhaps the eucharistic procession should be led by banners and accompanied by trumpets.

The elect immerse themselves completely in the paschal mystery of Christ made present. They become what they have received—the Body of Christ broken, the Blood of Christ poured out for the sake of the world. Having been washed, anointed and feasted, the neophytes are sent forth to go out and feed the world. Eucharist is our ongoing participation in Jesus' life—it is our continuing, repeatable sacrament of initiation.[2]

The neophytes are invited to return the next morning—Easter morning. They are a sign and a symbol of new life for all those who were unable to participate in the vigil, the primary feast of Easter. They remind the community of the new life in its midst. The neophytes, the "new shoots," dressed in white garments, baptismal candles in hand, process through the assembly and feast once again at the Lord's table. The presence of the neophytes at the eucharist on Sunday morning proclaims and unfolds the mystery of regeneration that took place the night before. On that same Easter Sunday morning liturgy, the catechumens still in process (those who were not initiated at the Easter Vigil) are dismissed with a catechist to break open the Easter scriptures and liturgy. Their dismissal is a powerful reminder that the work of evangelization and that the business of initiation in our communities is never finished. So begins the period of postbaptismal catechesis, mystagogia.

NOTES

1. The RCIA affirms that it is preferable that baptized candidates not celebrate the Rite of Reception into the Full Communion of the Catholic Church at the Easter Vigil in order to avoid confusion between the unbaptized and baptized candidates (NS, 33). The Easter Vigil is the night when the church gives birth through baptism. Anything that diminishes that focus is to be avoided. When there are more baptized candidates coming into full communion at the Easter Vigil, baptism is overshadowed. However, the RCIA also provides a combined rite in the event that pastoral circumstances dictate that the elect and baptized candidates complete their initiation together at the Easter Vigil. One instance in which this would be a pastoral necessity would be when within one family there are baptized and unbaptized persons seeking full initiation. In such a case, it is advantageous for the family to be received together rather than to defer a family member to another date in the Easter season. When celebrating a combined rite is recommended, it is important to be attentive to the distinctions between the baptized and the unbaptized.

2. For further elaboration on the Triduum refer to *Word and Worship Workbook, Cycles A, B and C* by Mary Birmingham (Paulist Press).

CHAPTER 9

Mystagogia

After being drenched in the five-foot-deep waters of baptism, Michael emerged from the font, into the waiting arms of the assembly. Dripping, exultant and with arms raised in the air, Michael shouted, "Thirty-five years of sin washed away!"

"When I tried to rub it in and rub off the globs of oil running down my cheeks and on my body," said Mary, "I realized what I had just done. I can't rub it off, but I can rub it in. I can't even wash it off—that really is what this is all about isn't it? I belong to God, signed, sealed and delivered!"

"I never knew how hungry I was," said Betty. "It was all so wonderful: the music, the stories, the word, the sharing, the people! For weeks I was becoming hungrier and hungrier. I thought the day would never come. I never really understood what true hunger meant before now. I know it now, because I know what it means to be filled!"

Memories laced with rich imagery and laden with deep meaning for their lives spark the imagination of the neophytes as they recall their initiation. Mystagogy provides the environment for this remembering. It is in the remembering that the saving action of Christ continues in their lives. Through the language of experience and poetry the neophytes break open the sacramental mysteries they celebrated at the Easter Vigil.

Originally, mystagogia was understood as the process of leading a recently initiated person into the sacred. The period of mystagogy, coinciding with the season of Easter, is a time for neophytes and the community to grow more deeply in their grasp of the paschal mystery—Jesus' life, death, resurrection, ascension and sending of the Spirit. This reflection is the agenda of all seven weeks of the Easter season. We do not refer to the Second Sunday *after* Easter. We refer, instead, to the Second Sunday *of* Easter. All seven weeks of Easter and Pentecost constitute the fullness of the Easter event. The postresurrection appearances are as much a part of the Easter story as the death and resurrection of Christ.

Mystagogia is not just the agenda of the Easter season. Celebration of and reflection on the paschal mystery is a lifelong, day-to-day concern in the life of Christians and the Christian community. Mystagogia is also a thread woven through the entire initiatory process. "Although formally placing mystagogy as last of the four stages, the Ordo implies a view of mystagogy that does not limit it to a final stage, but sees it as running through the whole process of initiation."[1]

The principle liturgy of the period of mystagogy is the Sunday eucharist. The entire community engages in mystagogical reflection on the paschal mystery and on our participation in that mystery. The purpose of the homilies of the Easter season is to crack open the mystery we celebrated at the Easter Vigil—the fullness of Christ's pasch made present and our participation in it. We grow in our grasp of this mystery through meditation on the gospel, sharing in the eucharist and doing works of charity (RCIA, 244), that is, by living the eucharistic life. By joining the community in these activities, the neophytes settle into their lives as fully initiated members.

The primary agenda of the period of mystagogy is fourfold: participation in and reflection on the Sunday liturgy (word and sacrament), participation in and reflection on the paschal mystery, living the eucharistic life and reflection on the symbols and sacramental mysteries of the Triduum. When that becomes the agenda of the entire parish there might be no need for further gatherings—the parish as a whole engages in mystagogy. Most places do not maintain that four-fold focus throughout the Easter season. In that event, supplemental gatherings of neophytes are important.

THE EASTER GOSPELS

The Year A gospels particularly speak to the neophyte's experience of initiation. If and when the neophytes begin to doubt their experience of presence and mystery, they have only to look to Thomas who had the same feelings. The story of Emmaus reminds the neophytes to continue their habit of mystagogical reflection on the experience of word and sacrament. Only then will they have the strength to return to Jerusalem and each day embrace the paschal mystery in their lives. When tempted to stray from the Master's voice, the neophyte recognizes the Good Shepherd who always searches for the lost. The neophyte continues to grow in his or her sacramental awareness of Jesus, the way, truth and life. The neophyte lives in the power and presence of Christ's Spirit and seeks a fuller outpouring of the Spirit's strength to continue the mission of Christ. The Year A readings embody the fullness of their sacramental life and serve as the blueprint by which they will build a life of committed discipleship.

While the Year A readings speak powerfully to the neophyte's experience of initiation and ongoing life, seldom does a parish use those readings exclusively every year. To do so would rob the parish of the scriptures from the other cycles. It is sometimes difficult, or at the very least challenging, for people in the period of mystagogy to concentrate on the Year A readings when the entire parish is reflecting on the scriptures of Year B or C. It behooves initiation ministers to discern whether or not to center the mystagogical reflection on the Year A readings, or whether to center on the scriptures of whatever cycle is celebrated in the parish.

It might be easier to use the Year A gospels if the neophytes meet during the period of mystagogy on a day other than Sunday. Gatherings might begin with a proclamation of a Year A gospel with a subsequent reflection on that gospel. Since the neophytes in my parish meet after Mass on Sunday morning, it is very difficult to reflect on the Year A gospel when the scriptures just proclaimed in Mass are from one of the other cycles. One way to address this problem is to provide the neophytes with material for home reflection. Each week they might be given the biblical citations of the Year A readings and a brief commentary to assist them in their prayerful reflection at home.

ACTS OF CHARITY

The crucial issue is not which gospel is proclaimed, but that the gospel deepens the neophyte's (and the entire community's) grasp of and participation in the paschal mystery. Mystagogical reflection naturally leads to a life of service and charity, which is also the hallmark of catechumenal formation. When parishes wait until the period of mystagogy to introduce neophytes to the apostolic life and corporal works of mercy, it is too late. Mission, service and charity are threads woven through the entire process. Apostolic formation begins in the precatechumenate. What is different about "acts of charity" during the period of mystagogy is that they are defined by the neophyte's participation in the eucharist. Nourished by the Bread of Life, the neophytes are sent out to feed others.

MYSTAGOGICAL CATECHESIS

The early centuries of the church enjoyed an advanced type of religious instruction which is known today as mystagogical catechesis—an introduction to the mysteries. This took place after—not before—baptism and was conducted by the bishop. It was believed that converts to Christianity were incapable of understanding the church's teaching on eucharist until they had undergone the experience. Once they had taken part in the eucharistic liturgy, then and only then would they be able to drink in the fullness of this awesome mystery. Perhaps an example will illustrate. A catechist preparing an engaged couple for marriage might talk about conjugal love—how it expresses love and commitment, how two become one body, its meaning for the sacrament of marriage, etc. But until the couple has the experience, they have only a cerebral understanding of what the catechist was teaching. Experience is the beginning of understanding. Saint Ambrose preached to the neophytes, "I shall begin now to speak of the sacraments which you have received. It was not proper for me to do so before this, because the Christian faith must come first."

Mystagogical catechesis weds truth and experience. During their preparation for baptism the catechumens immerse themselves in the truths emanating from their liturgical experience, they experienced the truths of our salvation history, and with baptism, confirmation and eucharist, they complete the rites of initiation. Now for the first time, the neophytes bring all their formation to bear—action, behavior, attitude and knowledge become one with the experience.

The sacraments of initiation are liturgical rites. They are experienced, celebrated and reflected upon. Appropriate connections are made and decisions for living flow from the experience. Mystagogy does not begin with Easter. As stated above, it should have been ongoing throughout the process of initiation. Candidates gathered for liturgy and for the celebration of liturgical rites. They experienced liturgy, ritual and word. They reflected on the experience and discovered meaning for their lives. They entered into the process of conversion. They allowed their habits, attitudes, behaviors, speech and actions to be touched by the transforming power of the Holy Spirit.

Scripture provides us with a vision of mystagogical catechesis. Consider the story of Emmaus. The disciples walk dejectedly from Jerusalem following the events of Calvary. They meet a stranger along the way. The stranger seems to be unaware of what happened. The disciples proceed to tell him. Their recounting is dripping with discouragement. Their hopes were dashed. They thought Jesus would be the one to deliver Israel.

Obviously frustrated with the disciples, the stranger explains the scriptures to them. He gives definition to the events of the last few days. He interprets the scripture for them, especially the texts that refer to him. Jesus explains the scriptures to them, which in turn prepares them to encounter him in the breaking of the bread. The scriptures were explained to the catechumens for a year of formation, which, in turn, prepared them to encounter Christ in the eucharist.

The stranger breaks bread with them. They recognize Jesus through the ritual action. They reflect on the experience. "Were not our hearts burning within us?" They understood the new, risen presence of Jesus. They enjoyed his physical presence before he died, now they experienced his risen presence. They were awed. Their awe prompted reflection. Their reflection led them to appropriate meaning for their lives. Their reflection led to action. They returned to Jerusalem without fear. There was work to be done, good news to tell. It was only in the context of ritual celebration that they were finally able to grasp not just the fact of the resurrection, but its meaning as well.

Neophytes experience the same type of mystagogical catechesis. Their understanding of scripture and the paschal life is taken to heart through the memory of water on the body, oil on the head, white garments worn, bread and wine feasted upon. When asked about her experience of eucharist, Sandy quickly responded, "I see it as maintenance." The curious response raised eyebrows until she continued: "When I was confirmed Christ was permanently sealed to my person. I cannot rub him off. Christ is indelibly imprinted on my soul. Eucharist is maintenance; it keeps me from ever breaking the seal."

The late Jim Dunning, founder of the North American Forum on the Catechumenate, asserted, "The catechists of mystagogy, who have themselves experienced the death and resurrection of Christ in their own lives, help new Christians transcend the Easter exaltation. They help the neophyte make the necessary connections with the Paschal Mystery. The cross they embraced at the Rite of Acceptance has given meaning to the dying they experience as they are plunged into the waters of baptism, thus taking on this new life of dying and rising."

Mystagogical catechesis invites us to take our experiences of death and resurrection, name them, reflect upon their meaning, and embrace a new world-view and way of relating in that world. This is catechesis par excellence. For the earliest Christian there was no distinction between catechesis and celebration. The agenda of mystagogy is to begin the lifelong habit of wedding celebration to catechesis—celebration which leads to reflection, which leads to meaning, which leads to decision for a transformed life. The neophytes point us to what we should all be doing. We are all to be practicing mystagogical reflection in our lives.

DEEPENING OUR GRASP OF THE MYSTERIES

Paragraph 245 of the RCIA notes that the neophytes are "introduced to a fuller and more effective understanding of mysteries through the Gospel message they have learned and above all through their experience of the sacraments they have received." The period of mystagogy is also referred to as the period of postbaptismal catechesis. This description offers the agenda of this period. The catechesis of this period leads the neophyte to a deeper appreciation and understanding of the mysteries encountered and celebrated at the Easter Vigil—the sacraments of baptism, confirmation and eucharist and their inherent symbols.

Through memory, the mysteries are brought into the present, and the neophyte echoes the meaning contained within them—a meaning gleaned from experience. Mystagogy is not a formal time for teaching about the sacraments or a course in sacraments 101. Rather, it is reflection upon the experience of sacraments. Saint Theodore believed that an explanation of each part of the liturgy is understood as a "theology of a mystery."[2] According to R. Tonneau and R. Devreese,

> Every mystery points in signs and symbols to things
> invisible and ineffable. A manifestation and explanation

of these signs and symbols is required if those who present themselves are to experience the power of the mysteries. If all that occurred was these actions, any discourse would be superfluous; the sight of them would be enough to make plain to us each thing that occurs. But since sacrament contains signs of what will take place or has already taken place, a discourse is needed that will explain the meaning of the signs and mysteries.[3]

Theodore, however, does not insist upon mystagogy on the sacraments for the sole sake of understanding sacramental theology. Rather, mystagogical catechesis heightens the awareness of and participation in the salvation and redemption the sacrament affords—salvation and redemption that will be complete only in the last times. It is an invitation to enter deeply into the mystery of Christ's saving love made present and ongoing in our sacramental life.

Mystagogical catechesis asks many questions: What did you experience? How do you understand the experience? How does your experience connect with how the church understands your experience? Are there any renewed insights that give meaning to your life? In what way was the risen Christ manifest to you in the celebration of the sacraments? In what way are you changed as a result? How will you live differently? How might you live as a better disciple as a result?

When the neophytes gather to remember the images of blazing fire, splashing water, fragrant oil, abundant bread and sumptuous wine, they recall the sacraments they received. Their experience speaks to them about God and God's relationship to his people. It is unnecessary to explain the sacramental mysteries away before they are experienced. To do so is to rob the sacrament of its power. When robust symbols are used that reveal the sacramental mystery (often without an uttered word), neophytes experience firsthand what we believe about the sacraments just celebrated.

Michael, who exclaimed, "Thirty-five years of sin washed away!" was not presented with a teaching about baptism. He was prepared to encounter the sacramental mystery fully and consciously by reflecting on our need for God's forgiveness due to sin, by praying scriptures that were baptismal in nature and by celebrating the rites leading up to his initiation. His experience of going down into the waters of death and resurrection was so powerful for him that the baptismal water communicated and revealed the liberation and washing that we teach baptism affords. The task of mystagogical catechesis for Michael was to affirm his experience and connect it with what Catholics believe about baptism. All we had to say to Michael was, "Wow, you just named a powerful truth we believe about baptism—the sacrament of baptism forgives sins. It is a person's first sacramental experience of having sins forgiven." Michael already knew that from his experience. The mystagogue, the person who leads the neophytes "into the divine mysteries,"[4] helps neophytes open their eyes to their experience—to help them name it and appropriate meaning for their lives. When liturgy is celebrated well, with robust symbols and proper preparation, it has the power to communicate divine reality. God is present and revealed in our symbols.

Many people misunderstand what Catholics believe about symbols. When the word *symbol* is used as a reference for eucharistic bread and wine they become somewhat agitated because they are appropriating a cultural definition of the word. Symbols not only point to, but also embody the sacramental mystery they reveal. The best way to understand what that means is to tell a story: The rabbi took a coin out of his pocket. He handed it to one of his students. "You see this coin. You not only see it, you can feel it. Right?" The rabbi then took the coin from the student, broke it in half and handed one half to his student. He hid the other half in his pocket. The rabbi proceeded to teach his student a profound truth about how a symbol functions. "You see the half you hold in your hand? You can see it, feel it and touch it. You can feel it with your senses. You know it exists. You also know that the other half of the coin exists. You cannot see it—it is hidden—but you know it exits. It is every bit as much a part of the reality—the truth of that coin—as the one you hold in your hand." That is how a symbol functions. There is a part that we can experience with our senses, and a part that remains hidden. The hidden part is the truth embodied in the sacramental symbol.

A symbol is something we have taken from everyday experience that reveals God to us. It embodies the truth it reveals. If a symbol could speak, it would not say, "I resemble that truth" or "I remind people of that truth." Rather, it would say, "I am that truth." If the symbol of bread could speak, it would not say, "I am like the Bread of Life," or "I remind people of Jesus' presence." The bread would say, "I am the Bread of Life. I am the presence of Christ." Oil would say, "I am the Spirit of God." Sacramental symbols not only express the sacramental truth, they embody it. Michael experienced the reconciling, transforming power of God through the waters of baptism.

The task of mystagogical catechesis is to tap the experience of the sacramental signs and to help the neophyte voice what the symbols reveal. Sandy's powerful experience of oil spoke to her of the permanence of Christ's Spirit in her life and the ongoing initiatory function of the eucharist. "Eucharist will keep me from ever breaking the seal." The function of mystagogy is to help the neophyte appropriate an understanding of eucharist that will help him or her begin a lifetime of plumbing its depths.

PRACTICAL CONCERNS

What then do neophytes do in the period of mystagogy? They continue what they have been doing throughout the process: celebrate liturgy, reflect on the experience, appropriate meaning and commit to ongoing transformation and live as disciples. No longer are they dismissed from the liturgy; they celebrate eucharist in the Sunday assembly. They are visible signs of new life. Each week of Easter they enter the church in the entrance procession of the Mass, carrying their baptismal candles and wearing their baptismal garments. They sit in a prominent place in the assembly. These folks, who left the assembly after the liturgy of the word for a year or more, now remain in the assembly. They are mentioned in the homily and the general intercessions. They are invited to process with their gifts for the poor and to bring the gifts of bread, wine and offering to the table. Perhaps they assist in preparing the table. All this is a striking contrast to the days when they were absent for the liturgy of the eucharist.

The neophytes are invited to witness to how they experienced the paschal mystery—the cycle of death and resurrection—throughout their initiation journey. A brief time might be allotted at the Sunday liturgies for this witness; if not, perhaps there are other parish gatherings where this might be appropriate. The period of mystagogy is a time for the neophytes to grow in their ability to evangelize. What better place to do that than in the parish community. Perhaps sponsors would witness to their experience of exercising their baptismal role as priest, prophet and king as they apprenticed this new life into community.

Mystagogy is not a time to assign neophytes to liturgical ministries in the parish. It is a time for them to grow in their understanding of the paschal mystery, to witness to the great deeds of God in their life and to live the eucharistic life. There is time for formal liturgical ministry as the neophyte becomes more comfortable in his or her role as a fully initiated member of the eucharistic community. Participation in ministries that reach out to the poor, sick and suffering, however, is appropriate. Such ministry is the heart of paschal living and should be a primary concern of neophytes for the rest of their Catholic lives.

Neophytes might support the ministry of initiation by witnessing to the inquirers or catechumens throughout the year if invited. They might assist and prepare social gatherings and receptions for catechumens and elect throughout the year as various rites are celebrated (acceptance/welcome, pre-election, Mardi Gras preparation for Lent, receptions following the vigil). Perhaps neophytes would offer prayers, support and letters of encouragement to catechumens as they journey through the process. The day will also come when the new Catholics will make wonderful sponsors or other ministers of initiation, but a period of mystagogy and settling into the Catholic community should take place first.

The neophytes gather during the Easter season to reflect on the Easter gospels in light of the paschal mystery and their eucharistic life. They also break open the symbols of the Triduum: the sacraments of baptism, confirmation and eucharist. Catechists for mystagogy must be imbued with an understanding of sacramental theology. Only then will they have the context with which to facilitate the neophytes' remembrances of the sacraments. Only then will they have ears with which to hear the cues, hints and hidden theologies expressed by the neophytes, remembrances. The job of the mystagogue is to wed experience to truth—to help the neophytes express a theology of their experience from the experience itself.

A special celebration and/or gathering is celebrated near the end of the Easter season, near the feast of Pentecost for the neophytes and their godparents. The neophytes also participate in a celebration of the eucharist in which the bishop presides at least once during the year; many dioceses celebrate such a liturgy each year.

The neophytes meet monthly for one year until the anniversary of their initiation "for their deeper Christian formation and incorporation into the full life of the Christian community" (National Statutes, 24). These gatherings could be situated around the sanctoral calendar. Many of the church's feasts and solemnities provide rich grist for celebration and mystagogical reflection. The new Catholics might desire a return to mysteries explored in the catechumenate for the purpose of gaining a deeper understanding of those mysteries. One way to continue to make the neophyte's presence known throughout the year is to call attention to the fact that they continue to meet. Perhaps the parish could be invited to participate in the experience of mystagogy with the neophytes, not just during the Easter season, but also throughout the year.

CHILDREN AND MYSTAGOGY

Everything that has been said about mystagogy applies to children as well. Children live in a world of symbols. They are phenomenal mystagogues. They see things adults long ago stopped seeing. Our parish gathers for an evening of remembrance shortly after the Easter Vigil. Everyone—both adults and children—brings pictures, baptismal gown and candle, videos, and we remember the night. We share stories and bring the memory into the present. We sing songs from the Triduum, read stories from scriptures and recall the reception of the sacraments. Everyone brings their handkerchief used for wiping the sweet scent of chrism from their foreheads. They remember their first communion. The children are wonderful participants. It is important that catechists who work with children participate in an evening such as this so that the children's presence is not overshadowed by an enthusiastic, extraverted adult community of neophytes.

Following the period of mystagogy, children continue their participation in the life of the community through the religious formation activities provided for children in the parish.

SAMPLE MYSTAGOGICAL SESSION

The following is one possible model for mystagogical catechesis that is useful throughout the process.

1) The neophytes remember and name their experience of a symbol, sacrament or other ritual moment.

2) Neophytes express their understanding of the symbol, sacrament or other moment.

3) Neophytes' experience is connected to the tradition of the church.

4) Neophytes have a conversation and test their experience and their understanding in light of tradition of the church. They discuss how their experience and the church's tradition invite a deeper participation into the paschal mystery.

5) Neophytes decide what the experience of symbol, sacrament, celebration, leading to meaning, challenges them to do, and what it will cost to do it.

MYSTAGOGY AND THE BAPTIZED CANDIDATE

How does a baptized person who has been received into the full communion of the Catholic church fit into mystagogy? An uncatechized, baptized person's formation parallels that of the unbaptized, uncatechized person. Thus, if mystagogy as described above is called for in the formation of the unbaptized, it is also called for in the formation of the baptized. The RCIA points to the formation of catechumens when it suggests the path for the uncatechized, unbaptized.

That does not mean, however, that baptized candidates will necessarily enter into full Catholic communion at the Easter Vigil. They may need a year of probation, but it need not parallel the Easter schedule. The baptized candidate is prepared to make a profession of faith and celebrate the sacraments of confirmation and eucharist. Their proximate preparation includes preparation for and the invitation to celebrate the sacrament of reconciliation. They enter into full Catholic communion whenever it is discerned that they are ready. Thus, the rite of reception is celebrated throughout the year at the Sunday liturgy. How, then, do they participate in mystagogy?

Every liturgical celebration is followed by mystagogical reflection throughout the process. Thus, baptized candidates who are brought into full communion enter into mystagogical reflection following the rite of reception. They might meet once or twice by themselves and then participate in the monthly mystagogy gatherings taking place throughout the year.

No matter what time of year the baptized candidates complete their initiation, they are invited to participate in the lenten baptismal and penitential preparations with the elect (as is the entire parish community). They are also invited to participate in mystagogy with the neophytes.

MYSTAGOGY AND SMALL CHRISTIAN COMMUNITIES

The candidates for initiation have been sharing life in the context of small group gatherings for an extended period of time. They are experts at it. Once they leave the catechumenal process, most of them miss the experience. There is no greater way to keep the fire alive than to continue to meet with other Christians to reflect on the Sunday scriptures. Even in situations where the parish does not support an active, small Christian community ministry, the neophytes could be encouraged to form their own small faith-sharing group. They could even provide the leaven for others in the parish to do the same.

MINISTRIES FOR MYSTAGOGY

CATECHIST

The best catechists for the period of mystagogy are those who are at home in the world of symbols. Teachers are not always good mystagogues. Poets and artists, however, might make wonderful catechists. The task of the mystagogue is to invite the neophyte to embrace mystery with renewed insight. The mystagogue has lived the paschal mystery and has the wisdom to invite others into the ongoing mystery of

Christ's death and resurrection. The mystagogy catechist's job is not to explain the mysteries away, but to allow the neophytes to discover for themselves what they experienced and how to weave that experience into their lives as a newly initiated member of the eucharistic community. New faces are needed—fresh catechists with fresh outlook and perspective. Perhaps catechists might be formed to minister only in the period of mystagogy. That would necessarily involve ministry for the weeks of Easter and once a month thereafter.

In smaller parishes or other ministry situations, it is important that the entire community engage in the business of mystagogy—Sunday liturgy and reflection on the paschal mystery. Formal ministry is not always the best ministry. If a parish is attentive to the vision of mystagogy it can take place right in the Sunday assembly. A few gatherings to share the experience of Holy Week might be all that is needed if the Sunday liturgy accomplishes what it is supposed to do.

If people are living the eucharistic life, they are doing mystagogy. There was a woman, a single parent, who was initiated at the Easter Vigil. She did not attend formal mystagogy gatherings. Upon further examination, though, it was discovered that she celebrated Sunday eucharist, was involved with her child's school and parish activities and volunteered one day each week, on her only day off, in a spousal abuse center. The woman was doing mystagogy!

PARISHIONERS

Mystagogy is everyone's business. Parish leaders should ask each year, In what ways does this parish break open the paschal mystery throughout the season of Easter? One way might be to invite parishioners, especially those who participated in the Triduum, to participate in gatherings for neophytes, to share their remembrances and to delve more deeply into the mysteries.

PRIESTS AND DEACONS

The primary mystagogical task of priests and deacons is to keep the paschal mystery before the community through their Sunday and weekday homilies and through their ministry in all aspects of parish life. Do the Easter season parish bulletins reflect a paschal focus? Does all ministry in the parish during the Easter season flow from a paschal context? In what way does parish ministry invite people more deeply into participation in the cycle of death and resurrection? Are parishioners reminded that every sacrament celebrates, remembers and makes present the paschal mystery of Christ? The Easter season is a good time to be reminded of that truth.

A FINAL WORD

Mystagogy shows how liturgy, celebrated to the full, embraced to the full, immerses neophytes and the church into the inexhaustible depths of the Christian mystery, the paschal mystery. Mystagogy uses the language of poets and the brush of the artist to paint the mysteries of the sacred on the soul and spirit of new Catholics.

Let us end with a mystagogical reflection on baptism inscribed on the fifth-century baptismal font of the church of St. John Lateran.

> Here is born in Spirit-soaked fertility
> a brood destined for another city,
> begotten by God's blowing and
> borne upon this torrent
> by the Church their virgin mother.
> Reborn in these depths,
> they reach for heaven's realm,
> the born-but-once unknown by felicity.
> This spring is life that floods the world,

the wounds of Christ

its awesome source.

Sinners sink beneath the sacred surf

that swallows age and spits up youth.

Sinners here scour sin away

down to innocence,

for they know no enmity who are

by one font, one Spirit,

one faith made one.

Sinners shudder not

at sins kind and number,

for those born here are holy.[5]

NOTES

1. Regan, David. *Experience the Mystery: Pastoral Possibilities of Christian Mystagogy.* Collegeville: The Liturgical Press, 1994, 31.

2. Mazza, Enrico. *Mystagogy,* New York, Pueblo Publishing Co., 1989, 53.

3. R. Tonneau and R. Devreese. *Les homélies catéchétiques de Theodore de Mopsueste,* ST 145 (Vatican City, 1949), XVI. Hom. 12, 2 (325).

4. Regan, 11.

5. Translation by Aidan Kavanagh.

Doctrine and the Catechumenate

Catechists sometimes reveal their frustration as they ask, How much doctrine equals "an appropriate acquaintance with dogmas and precepts" (RCIA, 75.1)? How much is too much and how much is not enough? What role does dogma play in the initiation of men, women and children? The *Rite of Christian Initiation of Adults* insists that doctrine plays a key role in the process of initiation. The vehicle by which doctrine is imparted in any setting, initiatory or otherwise, is referred to as catechesis. However, some believe that the word *doctrine* is synonymous with catechesis. The church sees it differently. Doctrine represents only a fraction of what catechesis implies.

What does the church mean when it refers to "a suitable catechesis" and "an appropriate acquaintance with dogmas and precepts" (RCIA, 75.1)? In order to shed light on the role of doctrine in the catechumenate, one must turn first to the text of the rite, but then one must also draw from other resources in our tradition to further understand this very complex subject. The *National Catechetical Directory* provides us with markers, as do the church's other catechetical documents, including the recent *General Directory for Catechesis.* The first task of this discussion is to explore the meaning of catechesis as it is described in the documents of the church, including the RCIA. Thus, we can determine where doctrine fits in the overall content of catechesis as prescribed for catechumenal catechesis.

CATECHESIS

In his 1979 apostolic exhortation *Catechesi Tradendae*, On Catechesis in Our Time (CT), Pope John Paul II reminds us that "at the heart of catechesis we find, in essence, the Person of Jesus of Nazareth. . . . Accordingly, the definitive aim of catechesis is to put people not only in touch but in communion, in intimacy, with Jesus Christ" (CT, 5). First and foremost, catechesis echoes the person of Jesus Christ and is primarily concerned with fostering an intimate relationship with God through Christ. One might conceivably be "educated" in the doctrines of the church and still not have experienced any meaningful level of conversion to Christ. Catechesis assumes as its goal a profound conversion to the person Jesus Christ.

SIGNS OF CATECHESIS

The church teaches that God is revealed to us through signs. *Sharing the Light of Faith: National Catechetical Directory for Catholics of the United States* (NCD), published by the bishops of the United States in 1978, reminds us that we are catechized by four signs of God's communication to the world (NCD, 41–46). God is revealed to us through natural signs, through our everyday lives, through creation, art, music, science and technology and through our experience of the world around us. Catechesis' aim is to help people encounter God in all creation and through the events of life. The NCD further reminds us that God is revealed through scripture (biblical signs); through the creed, life and mission of the church (ecclesial signs); and principally through the liturgy, the supreme celebration of the paschal mystery.

CATECHESIS ACCORDING TO THE GENERAL DIRECTORY

Before turning our attention to the RCIA itself, we must mention the *General Directory for Catechesis* (GDC), which was originally published by the Vatican in 1971 and was revised in 1997. The GDC situates all catechesis within the ministry of evangelization and uses the initiatory, conversion model of catechesis as the norm for all catechesis. Prior to this new document, the primary focus of catechesis was word and tradition. The revised GDC presents us with a huge paradigm shift, situating all catechesis within the apostolic ministry of evangelization. Initiation catechesis is a proclamation and living witness of the Good News of Jesus Christ; it falls under "promoting knowledge of the faith," one of the four fundamental tasks of catechesis enumerated in GDC, 85. It is an invitation to pray as Jesus prayed ("teaching to pray," 85). "When catechesis is permeated by a climate of prayer, the assimilation of the entire Christian life reaches its summit" (#85).

The GDC echoes similar church teaching when it insists that catechesis involves a gradual grasping of tradition and scripture and promotes an understanding of the liturgy and sacraments ("liturgical education," 85). Catechesis also forms disciples in a communal life of prayer, thanksgiving, reconciliation and repentance, and an understanding of the church's creed. It forms disciples to live a life in Christian community and to proclaim their faith to others in a spirit of ecumenism ("education for communal life," 86). Catechesis promotes moral transformation evidenced by a life lived in accord with the social demands of the gospel ("moral formation," 85). Catechesis forms people in a life of prayer, praise and apostolic service ("missionary initiation," 86).

CATECHESIS IN THE *RITE OF CHRISTIAN INITIATION OF ADULTS*

Our attention turns finally to catechesis in the catechumenate set forth in the RCIA. As mentioned earlier, the heart of all initiation catechesis is the paschal mystery of Christ. A primary focus of initiatory catechesis is evangelization and conversion. Catechumenal formation is multidimensional. It includes formation in the word (scripture and tradition), in worship (celebrated within the context of the liturgical year and the Sunday eucharist), in community (in which the community assumes its baptismal responsibility for initiation) and in service. This final formation is understood as apprenticeship in the life, mission and apostolic witness of the church (RCIA, 75).

LITURGICAL CATECHESIS

The RCIA reminds us that Catholic teaching is to be presented in its entirety (RCIA, 78), but that teaching must first and ultimately enlighten faith, invite an intimate relationship with God, promote conscious and active participation in the liturgy and inspire apostolic witness. Catechumenal catechesis should be adapted to liturgical signs. All catechesis prepares people for conscious and active participation in the liturgy and sacramental rites of the church, which are "the supreme celebrations of the paschal mystery" (NCD, 44). The RCIA insists that the "whole of initiation must bear a markedly paschal character, since the initiation of Christians is the first sacramental sharing in Christ's dying and rising" (RCIA, 8). Since liturgy is the sacramental sharing in the paschal sacrifice of Christ, liturgy is where primary catechumenal catechesis takes place. Liturgy proclaims the core creed of Christian faith; as the old axiom puts it, the rule of prayer constitutes the rule of belief—*lex orandi, lex credendi*. "If the aim of catechesis is to reveal Jesus Christ, the gospel that is proclaimed in the liturgy is the 'principle witness of the life and teachings of Jesus' " (NCD, 60). Thus, all catechesis flows from and leads to the celebration of liturgy, especially the Sunday eucharist, the seasons, feasts, solemnities and symbols of the liturgical cycle. Pope Pius XI stated it succinctly in his 1925 encyclical, *Quas Primas:*

> The annual celebration of the sacred mysteries is more effective in forming people about the spiritual life than the solemn pronouncements of the teaching Church. Documents are often read only by a few learned people; feasts move and teach all the faithful. The former speaks but once; the latter every year and forever. The former bring a saving touch to the intellect; the latter influence not only the mind but the heart and man's whole of human nature.

Thus, the primary locus of initiatory catechesis is the liturgical cycle and celebrations of the liturgy of the word. In one full liturgical cycle we remember and celebrate the life and mission of Christ from his incarnation through his passion, death, resurrection, ascension and sending of the Holy Spirit—the primary content of catechesis for sacramental initiation. For this reason the bishops of the United States insist that the catechumenate proper (not including the period of the precatechumenate) should extend for at least one complete liturgical cycle (RCIA, National Statutes, 6).

The first place where doctrine is encountered, therefore, is the Sunday liturgy of the word and other celebrations of the word prepared for the catechumens' formation (RCIA, 81). The primary documents for handing on that doctrine are the lectionary, the church's official collection of scriptures chosen for proclamation in the liturgy; and the sacramentary, the church's official book of prayers for the Mass.

The RCIA notes that one purpose of the celebration of the word is to implant the teachings of the church, such as the moral focus of the New Testament, the invitation to forgive injuries and insults, the understanding of the role of sin in one's life and the need for repentance (RCIA, 82.1). Celebrations of the word form catechumens in prayer, explain and break open the symbols of our faith and explore the meaning of that faith within the celebrations and seasons of the liturgy. The catechesis of this period is to help the catechumens to gradually learn to pray with the worshiping community (RCIA 82, 1–4). As the church prays the scriptures and ritual prayers of the liturgical year, as it shares the eucharist, it internalizes, professes and celebrates its belief in God, Jesus and Spirit, in the profound mystery of the church, and in Mary's preeminent role.

DISMISSAL CATECHESIS

The RCIA reminds the church to "kindly dismiss" (RCIA, 75.3) the catechumens so that they may "reflect more deeply upon the word of God" (#67 B), which they shared with the liturgical assembly. The *Catechism of the Catholic Church* reminds us that liturgy is the privileged home of catechesis and contains rich instruction for the faithful (CCC, 1074). Thus dismissed, catechumens engage in mystagogical reflection on the liturgy just celebrated: the liturgical season; the scriptures and their meaning (in dialogue with sound biblical scholarship); and the symbols, rituals and community. Mystagogical reflection leads to a decision for moral transformation as well as a commitment to share what they have celebrated and received with others—apostolic witness.

When one considers that the formation of catechumens takes place in one complete liturgical cycle, there need not be concern as to whether or not "Catholic teaching in its entirety"—all the doctrine—is presented. Not only is it presented in its entirety, but all the elements of catechumenal formation are allowed to gradually unfold—apprenticeship in the Christian life, growth in community, service and apostolic witness.

EXTENDED CATECHESIS

Sometimes reflection on the liturgy of the word ("breaking open the word") might lead to further, extended catechesis. The content for this extended catechesis might include further reflection: on church teaching, an evangelization-centered activity; an outreach of service and ministry to the poor; or parish activities such as retreats, missions or community-building events. The key to this extended catechesis is mystagogical reflection that asks the question, How does this extended session or activity invite growth as a discipled, missioned servant of Christ? When the liturgical season and the life of the community—not the school-year calendar—are the primary forces driving Christian initiation, all the elements of a "suitable catechesis" are given ample opportunity to emerge.

How is further "Catholic doctrine" presented? One cannot reflect on the liturgy and its scriptures week after week and not encounter the primary truths of our faith. Liturgy is where primary Christian doctrine is celebrated. When we break open the word, three factors determine the content for doctrinal catechesis: the liturgy just celebrated; the liturgical season and the theology it embodies; and the needs of the catechumenal community (RCIA, 81). When catechumenate teams provide their catechumens and candidates with a nine-month syllabus of doctrinal topics, there is a great risk of ignoring the most important criteria mentioned: the needs of the community.

Perhaps an example will illustrate the point. The six catechists in my parish meet monthly to reflect on scripture and tradition and to prepare for the coming weeks. At that time we prayerfully discern the needs of those who are in the catechumenate and we ask ourselves some very basic questions: Will the extended catechesis for the weeks of this month be a formal presentation of doctrine? Might we instead invite the catechumens and candidates to participate in a parish activity such as a parish mission, a retreat or an apostolic endeavor? What is going on in the lives of the catechumens and candidates? What doctrinal issues seem to naturally flow from each Sunday's liturgy of the word? Is there a strong insistence in the liturgy for definitive, corporate action? What will that corporate action be? Initiatory catechesis is apprenticeship. In what way have we apprenticed the catechumens and candidates this month? What is the liturgical season at hand, and are there any inherent doctrinal issues that we have yet to address? Are there any baptized candidates who will soon be celebrating a Rite of Reception into the Full Communion of the Catholic Church? Do they still have any unmet catechetical needs?

In an ideal world catechists would have the ability to ask the candidates and catechumens what doctrinal topic they would like to address based on their reflection on the liturgy of the word. However, we are not in that world yet and our catechists need time to prepare. In our parish, we tentatively determine the issues we will address for a few weeks in advance, with the understanding that we must be ready and willing to adapt. During one of our monthly preparation sessions, our catechists determined that the next week's liturgy invited a discussion on ecumenism. A catechist volunteered to facilitate the discussion. However, a call came in during the week from one of our candidates. His father was dying of cancer and his infant son was diagnosed with a catastrophic, fatal illness. Was a teaching on ecumenism still appropriate? Absolutely not. The catechist for that week was asked to switch gears and prepare a session on the paschal mystery. The result of that session was awesome. The catechumenal community volunteered to lift up that young man and his family throughout their entire ordeal. For the next year our catechumens, candidates, sponsors and catechists provided daily meals, helped with cleaning and lawn care so the family could spend every available moment with their dying son. Their efforts spilled out into the entire community. They were not only touched by our church's teaching on the paschal mystery, they embraced it and were profoundly transformed. Is that not the purpose of all catechesis? It is crucial that the needs of our catechumenate community be of primary importance when determining the content for extended catechesis.

Those who still want to know if Catholic teaching in its entirety is truly covered in the liturgical formation model of catechesis need only reflect on what the various seasons of the year echo and celebrate. The liturgies of Advent celebrate the reign of God; eschatology; and the coming of Christ in history, in our lives and at the Parousia. The season of Christmas celebrates the incarnation and manifestation of Christ, the Light of the world. We celebrate the fulfillment of salvation history; Mary, our disciple and model for the church; the holy family, Jesus' baptism and his mission. One need look no further than the prefaces for the Christmas season to find the most beautiful celebration of Catholic teaching on the incarnation of Jesus Christ. Lent celebrates baptismal, penitential and eucharistic preparation; conversion; the disciplines of prayer, fasting and almsgiving; moral transformation of sin in personal and social forms; and grace. Holy Week, the Easter Triduum and the Easter season celebrate, remember and make present the paschal mystery. Holy Week and the Easter season also celebrate our redemption, eucharist, baptism, confirmation, initiation, service, death and resurrection, salvation history, and justice. We celebrate the priesthood and the primary symbols of the church such as assembly, cross, light, water, oil, laying on of hands, garment, bread and wine. During the paschal season we celebrate the resurrection and ascension of the Lord, his postresurrection appearances, the Holy Spirit, the mission of the church, ecclesiology, discipleship, evangelization, Mary's role in the church and Pentecost. Ordinary Time (from the Latin ordinal, meaning "counted," not ordinary as in "humdrum") celebrates the entire mission of Jesus. Issues of faith which flow from the other 34 weeks of the year are paschal mystery, Trinity, eucharist, Christian witness, ecumenism, sacraments and sacramentality, the church's moral teaching, morality, moral decision making, Beatitudes, Creed, the Lord's Prayer, the Ten Commandments, vocation, stewardship, discipleship, communion of saints, death and resurrection, reign of God, and human dignity—to name but a few.

It is evident from the documents of our church that doctrine and dogma encompass more than formal instruction of systematically presented topics. Catholic dogma is crucial to our Catholic identity, but it includes so much more than merely passing on customs, content and "head" knowledge. It assumes a radical, lived and celebrated relationship with Jesus Christ that invites us into the cycle of death and resurrection so that we might, in turn, go out to die and live for others. At the heart of all doctrine is an invitation to live the radical call of discipleship. If we could fill our pews to capacity with parishioners well formed in word, worship, community, service and apostolic witness, the people of God would indeed be a formidable force and thus change the world!

From a Nine-Month Calendar to a Year-Round Catechumenate: Why Change?

The catechumenate is the church's nurturing womb of Christian generation and discipleship. Could such a metaphor, with its image of gestation and birth, be the subliminal reason many of us thought the catechumenate needed to be accomplished in nine months? Perhaps not, but the thought certainly teases the imagination! Or perhaps the nine-month schedule seemed right because the school model was tried, tested and proven successful, or because the school calendar has long established our culture's inner rhythm. It makes no difference. Perhaps the nine-month model served as a safe cradle that rocked the infant initiation process until it could stand on its own feet.

But now the initiation process we established just a few years ago has grown up. Now perhaps it is ready to stand tall and show forth the vision that was inherent in the rite all the time. Maria Montessori used to say that deep within each child is the adult he or she will one day become. This metaphor aptly describes the growth of Christian initiation in our time. Perhaps the nine-month school calendar model was a way to move from crawling to walking, but now it is time to embrace the maturity that has always lain just beneath the surface and enter fully into the "adult" stage of the rite of Christian initiation.

WELL DONE

How should we begin? First, we should pat ourselves on the back and tell ourselves, "Well done, good and faithful servants." We did a great job implementing the process the best we could and with the best intentions. We found ourselves meeting people and situations that did not fit into the tidy programs we had set up, and we responded by looking more deeply into the rite, finding what it really intends and how it is implemented. We had to ask:

> —What about the Patricks who come to us in January interested in becoming Catholic when our next inquiry group doesn't begin until next September?

> —What about the Kathys who come to us as cate-chized candidates needing only a brief period of sacramental catechesis, only to discover before the celebration of the Reception into the Full Communion of the Catholic Church that their parents forgot to have them baptized as children? Do we make them go through an entire catechumenate?

> —What about the Sarahs who come to us unsure of why they even came knocking at our doors in the first place, with God a nearly unknown factor in their lives? (One woman didn't even know that the figures of the woman, the man and the baby in the stable at Christmas time had anything to do with God!) People like these need a very gradual, and sometimes prolonged, evangelization. Do we provide a nurtur-ing place where they can take as long as they need in the precatechumenate to encounter the presence of the living God?

These are real people whom we meet, with real stories. They do not always fit into our neat and programmed packages. The RCIA had the vision to anticipate the Patricks, Kathys and Sarahs of this world in the very sacramental theology that informed the rite. Furthermore, the rite understood that Patrick's, Kathy's and Sarah's lifelong commitment to Jesus Christ depends on gradual formation and immersion into his life, death and resurrection and the sending of his Spirit at Pentecost. And the rite understood that some are already well immersed in that reality when they come knocking at our doors.

MAKING THE LEAP

Second, we must set aside our fears, and the excuses that come from such fears, and look at the reasons we resist making the radical shift needed in the way we initiate. Let us then have an honest talk with ourselves and say, "Get over it!" It's time to stop all the "yes, buts" and make the leap.

The challenges of operating a continuous year-round initiation process are minuscule in comparison to the leap that must first be made in ideology and assumptions. Such a leap demands that the theology that undergirds the initiation process be the deep foundation that sustains any structure we might create. We have to be willing to upset the "this is the way we've always done it" mentality.

At this point you may be asking, Why do I need to fix something I wasn't even sure was broken in the first place? Let us ask a few other questions to make a diagnosis:

>—Do we prepare our catechetical sessions by simply asking the catechumens to express their feelings about the readings without challenging anyone's assumptions or bringing transformative contemporary scholarship into the dialogue?

—Do the criteria we use to assign doctrinal topics have more to do with a need to "get it all covered" than with the connection of these topics to the liturgy of the day or the needs of the catechumenal communities?

—Are we providing a detailed syllabus and schedule of doctrinal topics and events to be covered between the First Sunday of Advent and the Easter Vigil?

If the answer to any of these is "yes," then we must take stock of our practices and realize that we might actually be engaged in religious education rather than in formation for initiation. Religious education is not bad; it is a very good thing. But it is not the agenda of the catechumenate. It is the agenda of an adult's entire lifetime. "Preparatory sacramental catechesis can be for a specified period of time—some weeks or months; the catechesis which follows is a life-long matter" (*National Catechetical Directory* [NCD], 36).

Paragraph 75 of the *Rite of Christian Initiation of Adults* reminds us that there are four dimensions to the formation we are to provide—catechetical, communal, liturgical and apostolic formation. The NCD reminds us that there are four signs of catechesis: that God is revealed through natural, biblical, ecclesial and liturgical signs. Is equal attention given to the presence of God through Christ in our everyday lives, through the stories of scripture and the interpretation of those stories, through the doctrines of the church and the way the church has lived its life of service and mission, and through the celebration of the liturgy? Is the initiatory catechesis we provide grounded in the tasks of catechesis set forth in the *General Directory for Catechesis,* numbers 85 to 86?

If attention is given primarily to ecclesial signs, that is, doctrine, then we are not providing the formation needed for a lifelong commitment to Jesus Christ in its fullness. We are not formed by doctrine alone. We are formed by living in the Christian community; by living the Christian life through our actions and apostolic works; by listening and acting upon the word of God and by recognizing the action of God in our everyday lives and allowing that action to transform us. Exploring the tradition that formed generations of disciples before us also forms us. We are formed by appropriating that tradition and by remembering, ritualizing and making present the words and actions of the Master and making those words and actions, his life, death and resurrection, our own. We are *finally* and continuously formed by taking our experience of Christ in the liturgy, in assembly, word and eucharist, with us into the world to further the reign of God in our everyday lives—to share the Good News with the entire world. When catechumens are not given the opportunity to apprentice in all those areas, we might be making great theologians, but are we making great disciples?

The church is so sure of the initiatory model of catechesis that it has situated all catechesis in the church within that context: "'The model for all catechesis is baptismal catechumenate when, by specific formation, an adult converted to belief is brought to explicit profession of baptismal faith during the Paschal Vigil.' This catechumenal formation should inspire the other forms of catechesis in both their objectives and in their dynamism" (GDC, 59).

If we do not carefully think through the underlying sacramental theology supporting an ongoing initiation process explored in the previous chapter, then a shift might involve nothing more than doing for twelve months what we managed to accomplish in nine. What is required is a radical shift in the way we do ministry as well as a renewed understanding of what informs the ministry we do. Therefore, before exploring strategies for implementation, it is necessary to become familiar with the theology that informs the rite.

PRAXIS VS. PRACTICE

Praxis involves the wedding of what we do (practice) with a theology that will inform and support it. People often groan, "Just tell us what to do and we will do it!" However, that often results in mechanical operation without the understanding needed to make creative and often necessary adaptations suited to the needs of the people we serve. It is sometimes easier simply to pick up a catechism than to create a fertile environment for a conversion-based model of sacramental catechesis. What, therefore, is the sacramental catechesis that undergirds this process? What is the theology that supports and informs the RCIA? What holds it all together? If we are to go through the work of changing from a nine-month model, which certainly seemed to get the job done, we need very good reasons.

CATECHESIS

First, we need to explore thoroughly a word that carries a myriad of meanings: *catechesis.* Very often we think of the word in narrow terms: the passing on of Catholic dogma. Pope John Paul II, in his apostolic exhortation *Catechesi Tradendae,* says, "the heart of catechesis is, in essence, a Person, the Person of Jesus of Nazareth, the only Son from the Father . . . who suffered and died for us, and who now, after rising, is living with us forever" (CT, 43). When we catechize, we reveal God's plan of salvation realized in the person of Jesus. Catechesis explores the meaning of Jesus' life, his words and his marvelous works. Catechesis is about relationship. It concerns a radical personal and communal relationship with the living God encountered in Jesus Christ through the Holy Spirit. "Catechesis helps us interpret the story of our lives in dialogue with the story of the scriptures and the story of the church throughout the ages."[1]

The catechesis we are talking about, a ministry of the word, is connected to Jesus' threefold mission: word, worship and service. Catechesis proclaims the Good News of Jesus Christ. It "leads to and flows from the ministry of worship . . . and supports the ministry of service" (NCD, 32). The purpose of catechesis is to make a person's faith come alive and grow into maturity, as evidenced by a life committed to constant conversion and renewal, to responsible Christian discipleship and to an active sacramental and prayer life (#33). "It implies education in knowledge of the faith and in the life of faith, in such a manner that the entire person, at his deepest levels, feels enriched by the word of God . . ." (GDC, 67). The *General Directory for Catechesis* insists that the fundamental task of initiatory catechesis is to promote knowledge of the faith, provide liturgical education, moral formation, teaching people to pray, formation in the life of the community and training in the apostolic life" (GDC 85–86). The infusion of Christian doctrine as the sole formation of catechumens and candidates limits their formation to just one part of the overall formation that is expected of any process of sacramental catechesis, and by itself does very little to promote the apostolic life.

Sacramental catechesis slowly forms and leads people over a period of time to experience and fully encounter the mystery inherent in the sacrament. Sacramental catechesis helps people encounter the sacraments in such a way that they will live a renewed, transformed life as a result of the sacramental experience. It is a process of conversion. Those preparing for sacraments—all the sacraments—are invited to turn their lives over completely to Christ. They connect the stories of their lives with the stories of salvation through Christ encountered in the scriptures, the sacraments and the liturgy. Linda Gaupin identifies the heart of this catechesis: The method used in sacramental catechesis is primarily to break open the meaning of the word, symbols and prayers found in the rite which reveal the nature of the sacramental mystery and to show how these relate to our lives. Religious education uses a variety of methods to form persons in the faith. The method for sacramental catechesis is based on Psalm 34. First we lead people to taste the Lord, and then we lead them to see.[2]

LITURGICAL CATECHESIS

> The catechumenate means not simply a presentation
> of teachings and precepts, but a formation in the
> whole of Christian life and a sufficiently prolonged
> period of training; by these means the disciples will
> become bound to Christ as their master.
> Catechumens should therefore be properly initiated
> into the mystery of salvation and the practices of
> gospel living; by means of sacred rites celebrated at
> successive times, they should be led gradually into
> the life, of faith, liturgy, and charity belonging to the
> people of God. (*Ad gentes,* 14)

The Catechism tells us that liturgy is the privileged home of catechesis. Catechesis flows from the liturgy and leads back to it again. The NCD insists that the celebration of the liturgy, the sacramental rites and the church year are important sources for catechesis (NCD, 44). The liturgy and the sacraments express and embody the heart of Christian faith—the paschal mystery of Jesus Christ. The liturgy celebrates the life, death and resurrection of Jesus in the word, symbols and gestures, and through the liturgical seasons of the year. "Within the cycle of a year, moreover, the church unfolds the whole mystery of Christ, from his incarnation and birth until his ascension, the day of Pentecost, and the expectation of blessed hope and of the Lord's return" (Constitution on the Sacred Liturgy [CSL], 102). The stories of Christ in the gospels, the Acts of the Apostles, the New Testament letters and the books of the Old Testament proclaimed in the celebration of the liturgy provide the primary formation in living the Christian life. The liturgy, liturgical seasons and feasts of the year provide a lens with which to view the mystery of Christ. The principle *lex orandi, lex credendi*—the law of prayer constitutes the law of belief—holds true.

The purpose of sacraments is to make people holy, to build up the Body of Christ and, finally, to give worship to God; being signs they also have a teaching function. They not only presuppose faith, but by words and objects they also nourish, strengthen and express it (CSL, 59).

Embodied in the prayer of the church is the doctrine we profess. One need only turn to the preface for the seasons of Advent and Christmas for an articulation of our theology of Advent and of what the incarnation of Christ means for a waiting world. In one complete liturgical cycle the truths of the faith are set out in the celebration of the liturgy and the proclamation of the word. The liturgy provides formation centered on the word of God and on the liturgy itself. As the RCIA points out, "Catechists, when they are teaching, should see that their instruction is filled with the spirit of the gospel, adapted to liturgical signs and the cycle of the church's year, and suited to the needs of catechumens" (RCIA, 16).

SUITED TO CATECHUMENS

The liturgy, readings, symbols, ritual prayers and gestures in the context of the liturgical year set forth the truths of our faith, but this is not done in a sterile or static fashion. It takes place in a community that has its own story and in the lives of catechumens with similar stories. Thus, in any liturgy, there might be several doctrinal themes that emerge, but only one fits a specific community at a specific time in specific circumstances. Perhaps the scriptures and prayers of a certain liturgy speak clearly of a certain doctrinal topic such as conversion, but at that specific time the community is concerned about a tragedy in its life. It is likely that the community will be more aware of another doctrinal theme echoing in that specific liturgy: the mystery of Christ's suffering, death and resurrection inherent in every liturgical or sacramental celebration. The doctrinal agenda is driven by the needs of the celebrating and catechumenal community. Flexibility must be built into the process.

WHY A CONTINUOUS CATECHUMENATE?

Why should we change to a year-round catechumenate? The rite itself sets forth the rationale. We are reminded in the RCIA that the catechumenate is an extended period of formation and guidance aimed at training the catechumens in the Christian life (RCIA, 74). We are further exhorted to provide a suitable catechesis for catechumens that is gradual, thorough and accommodated to the liturgical year (#75). We are also reminded that the length of the catechumenate will depend on God's grace and various circumstances. The catechumenate is intended to last as long as necessary for faith and conversion to take root in the lives of catechumens—several years, if necessary. By virtue of their formation in the Christian life and an extended period of searching, catechumens are initiated into the sacramental mystery of salvation as well as the church's apostolic life (#76). The catechumenate is expected to last "a substantial and appropriate period of time" (#20). The period of the catechumenate proper, from the celebration of the Rite of Acceptance until the celebration of the initiation sacraments at the Easter Vigil, is to extend at least one full year for unbaptized, uncatechized persons.

The period of the catechumenate, beginning at acceptance into the order of catechumens and including both the catechumenate proper and the period of purification and enlightenment after election or the enrollment of names, should extend for at least one year of formation, instruction and probation. Ordinarily this period should go from at least the Easter season of one year until the next; preferably it should begin before Lent in one year and extend until Easter of the following year (National Statutes, 6).

Nowhere in the rite is there even a hint that the initiation of catechumens is to take nine months. Nor does the RCIA suggest that there be only one celebration of the Rite of Acceptance on or around the First Sunday of Advent, thereby creating a three- or four-month catechumenate:

> The rite of acceptance should not be too early, but should be delayed until the candidates . . . have had sufficient time to conceive an initial faith and to show the first signs of conversion. Two dates in the year, three if necessary, are to be fixed as the usual times for carrying out this rite. (RCIA, 18)

Finally, the RCIA insists that the Rite of Acceptance into the Order of Catechumens is to take place when the time is right (RCIA, 28).

It is clearly the intention of the rite that the formation of catechumens be a gradual process of conversion, marked by the celebration of liturgical rites. This formation is to take as long as needed for catechumens to be formed and absorbed into the life, death and resurrection of Jesus Christ and his church as experienced and celebrated in the liturgy in one complete year-long cycle. While the presentation of Catholic dogma is certainly a piece of the process, it is not the basis of it. The agenda of a content-only model of the catechumenate is that every Catholic precept be taught because this is the first, last and only time we will see the catechumens. This attitude may stem from inadequate structures for adult education in the parish, prompting the idea that we need to teach catechumens what it really takes a lifetime to learn because we will never have this captive audience again.

Without a shift from religious education to a formation-centered initiation process, it makes little difference to change from a school-year model to a liturgical-year model. As stated before, that would simply extend for twelve months what we were accomplishing in nine. The heart of the year-round model is concerned with our understanding of catechesis. Is catechesis understood as content or relationship? Is our primary goal the imparting of Catholic doctrine, or the mentoring of committed, gospel-living disciples? The RCIA embraces dogma as a piece of its vision. But dogma always leads to the question, How does this piece of tradition invite me to be a mature, transformed disciple committed to living and sharing the Good News of Jesus Christ?

A return to the opening metaphor reminds us that this is a process of birth. In life, giving birth involves care, patient waiting and intense labor before a new life comes forth. The process of Christian initiation involves our ongoing care, patient waiting and serious attention. It goes without saying that intense labor is part of the process. Christians are anointed priest, prophet and ruler at baptism. It is our baptismal mandate, therefore, to labor in the service of God's people, to preach the living word of God and to lead people to Christ. A formation-centered model of sacramental catechesis cannot merely be an option. It is the only way we can accomplish what our baptism demands.

NOTES

1. Mary Birmingham. *Word and Worship Workbook for Year C* (New York: Paulist, 1997).

2. Linda Gaupin, CDP, PhD. "Sacramental Catechesis, Part III: A Blueprint for Sacramental Catechesis," *Total Religious Education Newsletter* 2 (November 1997): 5.